THIS BOOK BELONGS TO

_____

START DATE

_____

SHE READS TRUTH

FOUNDERS

FOUNDER
Raechel Myers

CO-FOUNDER
Amanda Bible Williams

EXECUTIVE

CHIEF EXECUTIVE OFFICER
Ryan Myers

CHIEF BRAND & MARKETING OFFICER
Amy Dennis

CHIEF CONTENT OFFICER
Jessica Lamb

CHIEF OPERATING OFFICER
Raechel Myers

EDITORIAL

PRODUCTION EDITOR
Hannah Little, MTS

MARKETING CONTENT EDITOR
Tameshia Williams, ThM

ASSOCIATE EDITORS
Kayla De La Torre, MAT
Lindsey Jacobi, MDiv

COPY EDITOR
Becca Owens, MA

MARKETING

MARKETING PROJECT COORDINATOR
Kyndal Kearns

GROWTH MARKETING MANAGER
Blake Showalter

PRODUCT MARKETING MANAGER
Whitney Hoffman

SOCIAL MEDIA STRATEGIST
Taylor Krupp

CREATIVE

DESIGN MANAGER
Kelsea Allen

DESIGNERS
Abbey Benson
Amanda Brush, MA
Annie Glover
Lauren Haag

JUNIOR DESIGNER
Jessie Gerakinis

OPERATIONS

OPERATIONS DIRECTOR
Allison Sutton

OPERATIONS COORDINATORS
Nicole Quirion
Mary Beth Steed

SHIPPING

SHIPPING MANAGER
Marian Byne

FULFILLMENT LEAD
Cait Baggerman

FULFILLMENT SPECIALIST
Hannah Lamb
Kajsa Matheny
Lauren Neal

SUBSCRIPTION INQUIRIES
orders@shereadstruth.com

COMMUNITY SUPPORT

COMMUNITY EXPERIENCE DIRECTOR
Kara Hewett, MOL

COMMUNITY SUPPORT SPECIALISTS
Katy McKnight
Alecia Rohrer
Heather Vollono

CONTRIBUTORS

PHOTOGRAPHY
Becca Cannon (78)
Katherine Joy (16, 44, 60, 82, 106)

SPECIAL THANKS
Russ Ramsey
Kara Gause
Melanie Rainer
Ellen Taylor
Emily Knapp
Kamron Kunce
Oghosa Iyamu, MDiv

SHE READS TRUTH™

© 2018, 2023 by She Reads Truth, LLC
All rights reserved. First edition 2018.
Second edition 2023.

All photography used by permission.

ISBN 978-1-952670-89-3

1 2 3 4 5 6 7 8 9 10

All Scripture is taken from the Christian Standard Bible®. Copyright © 2020 by Holman Bible Publishers. Used by permission. Christian Standard Bible® and CSB® are federally registered trademarks of Holman Bible Publishers.

Though the dates in this book have been carefully researched, scholars disagree on the dating of many biblical events.

Research support provided by Logos Bible Software™. Learn more at logos.com.

This book was printed offset in Nashville, Tennessee, on 70# Lynx Opaque. Cover is 100# Cougar Opaque with a soft touch lamination.

@SHEREADSTRUTH

 Download the She Reads Truth app, available for iOS and Android

  Subscribe to the She Reads Truth podcast

JUDGES

THE TRAGEDY OF FORGETTING GOD

Forgetting the one true God—both His goodness and His holiness—is a tragedy.

Jessica

Jessica Lamb
CHIEF CONTENT
OFFICER

I still remember the misguided giddiness I felt when my eighth grade English teacher announced we would be reading Shakespeare's *Romeo and Juliet*. I knew little of the titular star-crossed lovers or of Shakespeare beyond that the work was something famous I should read and appreciate.

I was livid when I read the end of the play. Romeo and Juliet were both dead, and there was no happily ever after. What sort of love story was this?

It isn't one, really. It's a tragedy. Every twist and turn that leads to the demise of the young couple is meant to bring an ache to our hearts, because we realize how easily it could have been avoided. We're meant to be outraged at the selfish actions of the Capulets and Montagues, and we're meant to feel upset and distressed at the ending. That's how tragedy works. (For more on this genre, look ahead to "What Is a Tragedy?" on page 104.)

The book of Judges is the tragic, true story of the people of Israel ignoring God's instructions and abandoning their faith to live like their pagan neighbors. With each new judge, it documents a downward cycle of rebellion and rescue as Israel moves from obedience to bleak despair. More often than not, the actions on the page are horrifying, dripping with rebellion and violence.

Forgetting the one true God—both His goodness and His holiness—is a tragedy. We hope for God's people to get it right with each new rescue God provides. But the final scenes of this book are tragic. It just ends, with everyone doing whatever seemed right to them. As readers, we're left with a sense of longing for how things ought to be.

In this book, we endeavored to present the text of the book of Judges in a way that is accessible and thoughtful without masking the sobering reality of these events in Scripture. We used infographics and charts to give context to what was happening culturally and spiritually in Israel. The "Joshua, Judges, Ruth" extra on page 16 shows where Judges fits in the surrounding story of the Bible, highlighting the seed of hope that took root in a foreign widow's decision to follow God during the time of the judges. You'll find Psalm 32, a psalm celebrating forgiveness, spread across Grace Days as a moment to rest in the hope that is ours because of God's grace.

I pray that as you read, you will discover the source of true redemption in these pages. We can draw hope from the fact that God continues to work through broken, morally compromised, deeply flawed people and circumstances. He isn't limited by our shortcomings. He isn't limited by the brokenness in our world. His story—and because of Him, our story—is not one of tragedy but one of profound beauty and hope in Jesus Christ. Thanks be to God.

DESIGN ON PURPOSE

At She Reads Truth, we believe in pairing the inherently beautiful Word of God with the aesthetic beauty it deserves. Each of our resources is thoughtfully and artfully designed to highlight the beauty, goodness, and truth of Scripture in a way that reflects the themes of each curated reading plan.

When designing this book, we wanted to respect the somber subject matter while preserving God's promise of hope in the darkness. We used bold contrasts within this book's photography and color scheme to illustrate how deep Israel's rebellion is in contrast to the steadfast love and mercy of God.

The photography throughout this book features dramatic shadows and light, underscoring both the Israelites' lack of vision when they turned away from God and the power God's light has in dark places. We paired dark navy and black shades to match the tone of the images and stories in the book of Judges, breaking into lighter beiges on the Grace Days to instill hope.

As you read, we hope the design of this book allows you to be present with the events of the book of Judges while also allowing you to see God's redeeming presence on every page.

HOW TO USE THIS BOOK

She Reads Truth is a community of women dedicated to reading the Word of God every day. In this **Judges** reading plan, we will read Judges, along with complementary passages of Scripture, as we grieve the tragedy of sin and cling to the hope of Jesus.

READ & REFLECT

Your **Judges** book focuses primarily on Scripture, with added features to come alongside your time with God's Word.

SCRIPTURE READING

Designed for a Monday start, this book presents the book of Judges in daily readings, along with additional passages curated to show how the theme of the main reading can be found throughout Scripture.

🔖 *Additional passages are marked in your daily reading with the Going Deeper heading.*

JOURNALING SPACE

Each weekday features space for personal reflection and prayer.

COMMUNITY & CONVERSATION

You can start reading this book at any time! If you want to join women from Montpelier to Malaysia as they read along with you, the She Reads Truth community will start Day 1 of **Judges** on Monday, October 16, 2023.

 SHE READS TRUTH APP

Devotionals corresponding to each daily reading can be found in the **Judges** reading plan on the She Reads Truth app. Devotionals will be published each weekday once the plan begins on Monday, October 16, 2023. You can use the app to participate in community discussion and more.

GRACE DAY

Use Saturdays to catch up on your reading, pray, and rest in the presence of the Lord.

WEEKLY TRUTH

Sundays are set aside for Scripture memorization.

See tips for memorizing Scripture on page 124.

EXTRAS

This book features additional tools to help you gain a deeper understanding of the text.

Find a complete list of extras on pages 10–11.

 SHEREADSTRUTH.COM

The **Judges** reading plan and devotionals will also be available at SheReadsTruth.com as the community reads each day. Invite your family, friends, and neighbors to read along with you!

 SHE READS TRUTH PODCAST

Subscribe to the She Reads Truth podcast and join our founders and their guests each week as they talk about what you'll read in the week ahead.

 *Podcast episodes 195–198 for our **Judges** series release on Mondays beginning October 16, 2023.*

TABLE OF CONTENTS

The Judges of Israel
PAGE 90

What Is a Tragedy?
PAGE 104

For the Record
PAGE 128

KEY / VERSE

In those days there was no king in Israel;
everyone did whatever seemed right to him.

JUDGES 21:25

JUDGES: THE TRAGEDY OF FORGETTING GOD

SHE READS JUDGES

ON THE TIMELINE

The period of the Israelite judges took place between the conquest of the promised land under Joshua and the rise of the monarchy with Saul and David. The events can be safely dated from the beginning of the fourteenth century BC to the middle of the eleventh century BC, a period of about three hundred years (approximately 1380 BC to 1050 BC).

A LITTLE BACKGROUND

It is unclear when the book of Judges was written. The Assyrian captivity of Israel is referenced in 18:30, which suggests a date of final editing after the exile of the northern kingdom in 722 BC. But the implication of 6:24, that readers could visit the site of Gideon's altar at Ophrah, suggests a final editing date before the exile of the southern kingdom, Judah, in 586 BC. The message of Judges would have resonated strongly from 697–642 BC during the dark days of Manasseh (2Kg 21), though the same could be said for several points in Israel's history. Even considering this information, it is not possible to assign an exact date to the writing of this book.

MESSAGE & PURPOSE

The book of Judges chronicles the moral and spiritual descent of Israel, from the relative high point at the beginning of the book through a series of downward spirals into the depths of degradation in chapters 17–21. Though God raised up a sequence of deliverers—the judges—they were unable to reverse this trend and some even became part of the problem themselves. By the end of the book, Israel had become as pagan and defiled as the Canaanites around them.

GIVE THANKS FOR THE BOOK OF JUDGES

The book of Judges shows us that the nation of Israel survived the dark days of the judges entirely by the grace of God. In mercy, He sent oppressors as reminders of their rebellion. In mercy, He responded to their cries and raised up deliverers. Judges illustrates the fundamental problem of the human heart: when God's people forget His saving acts, they go after other gods. In the end, the book of Judges illustrates an eternal truth: the Lord will build His kingdom, in spite of our sin and rebellion.

JOSHUA, JUDGES, RUTH

To understand the book of Judges, it helps to remember its place in Israel's history. The book of Judges comes directly in between the books of Joshua and Ruth in the Protestant Bible. Though Judges reads as a tragedy on its own, the combined books of Joshua, Judges, and Ruth tell a story of great hope.

JOSHUA

In the book of Joshua, the Israelites are repeatedly called to worship the Lord and serve Him only.

After God's people endured over four hundred years in Egypt, followed by forty years of wandering in the wilderness, the Lord raised up Joshua to lead Israel into the promised land.

Joshua led a successful conquest, Israel took the land of Canaan, and the twelve tribes began to settle there.

Therefore, fear the LORD and worship him in sincerity and truth. Get rid of the gods your ancestors worshiped beyond the Euphrates River and in Egypt, and worship the LORD. But if it doesn't please you to worship the LORD, choose for yourselves today: Which will you worship—the gods your ancestors worshiped beyond the Euphrates River or the gods of the Amorites in whose land you are living? As for me and my family, we will worship the LORD.

JOSHUA 24:14–15

JUDGES

Judges describes how Israel rejected the Lord and adopted the worship practices of the Canaanites.

Israel experienced chaotic and catastrophic consequences due to their rebellion. This period was marked by repeated cycles of unprecedented violence and oppression.

God raised up judges to rescue the Israelites from the oppression of enemies, but the cycle of sin continued.

Israel's downward spiral of rebellion led them to become almost unrecognizable as the people of God.

In those days there was no king in Israel; everyone did whatever seemed right to him.

JUDGES 21:25

RUTH

In the book of Ruth, a Moabite woman embraces the God of Israel.

During the time of the judges, famine sent Naomi's family away from Bethlehem to Moab, where one of her sons married a Moabite woman named Ruth.

When Naomi and Ruth were widowed, Ruth, a Moabite, pledged to stay with Naomi, an Israelite, and follow the God of Israel.

Ruth married an Israelite named Boaz and gave birth to Obed, King David's grandfather. From the line of Ruth and David would come Jesus, the Savior of the world.

Blessed be the LORD, who has not left you without a family redeemer today. May his name become well known in Israel.

RUTH 4:14

THE FAILURE
OF THE TRIBES

JUDGES 1

Judah's Leadership Against the Canaanites

¹ After the death of Joshua, the Israelites inquired of the Lord, "Who will be the first to fight for us against the Canaanites?"

² The Lord answered, "Judah is to go. I have handed the land over to him."

³ Judah said to his brother Simeon, "Come with me to my allotted territory, and let's fight against the Canaanites. I will also go with you to your allotted territory." So Simeon went with him.

⁴ When Judah attacked, the Lord handed the Canaanites and Perizzites over to them. They struck down ten thousand men in Bezek. ⁵ They found Adoni-bezek in Bezek, fought against him, and struck down the Canaanites and Perizzites.

⁶ When Adoni-bezek fled, they pursued him, caught him, and cut off his thumbs and big toes. ⁷ Adoni-bezek said, "Seventy kings with their thumbs and big toes cut off used to pick up scraps under my table. God has repaid me for what I have done." They brought him to Jerusalem, and he died there.

⁸ The men of Judah fought against Jerusalem, captured it, put it to the sword, and set the city on fire. ⁹ Afterward, the men of Judah marched down to fight against the Canaanites who were living in the hill country, the Negev, and the Judean foothills. ¹⁰ Judah also marched against the Canaanites who were living in Hebron (Hebron was formerly named

Kiriath-arba). They struck down Sheshai, Ahiman, and Talmai. ¹¹ From there they marched against the residents of Debir (Debir was formerly named Kiriath-sepher).

¹² Caleb said, "Whoever attacks and captures Kiriath-sepher, I will give my daughter Achsah to him as a wife." ¹³ So Othniel son of Kenaz, Caleb's youngest brother, captured it, and Caleb gave his daughter Achsah to him as his wife.

¹⁴ When she arrived, she persuaded Othniel to ask her father for a field. As she got off her donkey, Caleb asked her, "What do you want?" ¹⁵ She answered him, "Give me a blessing. Since you have given me land in the Negev, give me springs also." So Caleb gave her both the upper and lower springs.

¹⁶ The descendants of the Kenite, Moses's father-in-law, had gone up with the men of Judah from the City of Palms to the Wilderness of Judah, which was in the Negev of Arad. They went to live among the people.

¹⁷ Judah went with his brother Simeon, struck the Canaanites who were living in Zephath, and completely destroyed the town. So they named the town Hormah. ¹⁸ Judah captured Gaza and its territory, Ashkelon and its territory, and Ekron and its territory. ¹⁹ The Lord was with Judah and enabled them to take possession of the hill country, but they could not drive out the people who were living in the plain because those people had iron chariots.

²⁰ Judah gave Hebron to Caleb, just as Moses had promised. Then Caleb drove out the three sons of Anak who lived there.

Benjamin's Failure

²¹ At the same time the Benjaminites did not drive out the Jebusites who were living in Jerusalem. The Jebusites have lived among the Benjaminites in Jerusalem to this day.

Success of the House of Joseph

²² The house of Joseph also attacked Bethel, and the Lord was with them. ²³ They sent spies to Bethel (the town was formerly named Luz). ²⁴ The spies saw a man coming out of the town and said to him, "Please show us how to get into town, and we will show you kindness." ²⁵ When he showed them the way into the town, they put the town to the sword but released the man and his entire family. ²⁶ Then the man went to the land of the Hittites, built a town, and named it Luz. That is its name still today.

Failure of the Other Tribes

²⁷ At that time Manasseh failed to take possession of Beth-shean and Taanach and their surrounding villages, or the residents of Dor, Ibleam, and Megiddo and their surrounding villages; the Canaanites were determined to stay in this land. ²⁸ When Israel became stronger, they made the Canaanites serve as forced labor but never drove them out completely.

²⁹ At that time Ephraim failed to drive out the Canaanites who were living in Gezer, so the Canaanites have lived among them in Gezer.

³⁰ Zebulun failed to drive out the residents of Kitron or the residents of Nahalol, so the Canaanites lived among them and served as forced labor.

³¹ Asher failed to drive out the residents of Acco or of Sidon, or Ahlab, Achzib, Helbah, Aphik, or Rehob. ³² The Asherites lived among the Canaanites who were living in the land, because they failed to drive them out.

³³ Naphtali did not drive out the residents of Beth-shemesh or the residents of Beth-anath. They lived among the Canaanites who were living in the land, but the residents of Beth-shemesh and Beth-anath served as their forced labor.

³⁴ The Amorites forced the Danites into the hill country and did not allow them to go down into the valley. ³⁵ The Amorites were determined to stay in Har-heres, Aijalon, and Shaalbim. When the house of Joseph got the upper hand, the Amorites were made to serve as forced labor. ³⁶ The territory of the Amorites extended from the Scorpions' Ascent, that is from Sela upward.

◆ GOING DEEPER

DEUTERONOMY 30:15–20

¹⁵ See, today I have set before you life and prosperity, death and adversity. ¹⁶ For I am commanding you today to love the LORD your God, to walk in his ways, and to keep his commands, statutes, and ordinances, so that you may live and multiply, and the LORD your God may bless you in the land you are entering to possess. ¹⁷ But if your heart turns away and you do not listen and you are led astray to bow in worship to other gods and serve them, ¹⁸ I tell you today that you will certainly perish and will not prolong your days in the land you are entering to possess across the Jordan. ¹⁹ I call heaven and earth as witnesses against you today that I have set before you life and death, blessing and curse. Choose life so that you and your descendants may live, ²⁰ love the LORD your God, obey him, and remain faithful to him. For he is your life, and he will prolong your days as you live in the land the LORD swore to give to your ancestors Abraham, Isaac, and Jacob.

PSALM 32
The Joy of Forgiveness
Of David. A Maskil.

¹ How joyful is the one
whose transgression is forgiven,
whose sin is covered!
² How joyful is a person whom
the LORD does not charge with iniquity
and in whose spirit is no deceit!

³ When I kept silent, my bones became brittle
from my groaning all day long.
⁴ For day and night your hand was heavy on me;
my strength was drained
as in the summer's heat.   *Selah*
⁵ Then I acknowledged my sin to you
and did not conceal my iniquity.
I said, "I will confess my transgressions to the LORD,"
and you forgave the guilt of my sin.   *Selah*

⁶ Therefore let everyone who is faithful pray to you immediately.
When great floodwaters come,
they will not reach him.
⁷ You are my hiding place;
you protect me from trouble.
You surround me with joyful shouts of deliverance.   *Selah*

⁸ I will instruct you and show you the way to go;
with my eye on you, I will give counsel.
⁹ Do not be like a horse or mule,
without understanding,
that must be controlled with bit and bridle
or else it will not come near you.

¹⁰ Many pains come to the wicked,
but the one who trusts in the LORD
will have faithful love surrounding him.
¹¹ Be glad in the LORD and rejoice,
you righteous ones;
shout for joy,
all you upright in heart.

What have you done?

JUDGES 2:2

SIN AND JUDGMENT

JUDGES 2
Pattern of Sin and Judgment

[1] The angel of the LORD went up from Gilgal to Bochim and said, "I brought you out of Egypt and led you into the land I had promised to your ancestors. I also said: I will never break my covenant with you. [2] You are not to make a covenant with the inhabitants of this land. You are to tear down their altars. But you have not obeyed me. What have you done? [3] Therefore, I now say: I will not drive out these people before you. They will be thorns in your sides, and their gods will be a trap for you." [4] When the angel of the LORD had spoken these words to all the Israelites, the people wept loudly. [5] So they named that place Bochim and offered sacrifices there to the LORD.

Joshua's Death

[6] Previously, when Joshua had sent the people away, the Israelites had gone to take possession of the land, each to his own inheritance. [7] The people worshiped the LORD throughout Joshua's lifetime and during the lifetimes of the elders who outlived Joshua. They had seen all the LORD's great works he had done for Israel.

[8] Joshua son of Nun, the servant of the LORD, died at the age of 110. [9] They buried him in the territory of his inheritance, in Timnath-heres, in the hill country of Ephraim, north of Mount Gaash. [10] That whole generation was also gathered to their ancestors. After them another generation rose up who did not know the LORD or the works he had done for Israel.

¹¹ The Israelites did what was evil in the Lord's sight. They worshiped the Baals ¹² and abandoned the Lord, the God of their ancestors, who had brought them out of Egypt. They followed other gods from the surrounding peoples and bowed down to them. They angered the Lord, ¹³ for they abandoned him and worshiped Baal and the Ashtoreths.

¹⁴ The Lord's anger burned against Israel, and he handed them over to marauders who raided them. He sold them to the enemies around them, and they could no longer resist their enemies. ¹⁵ Whenever the Israelites went out, the Lord was against them and brought disaster on them, just as he had promised and sworn to them. So they suffered greatly.

¹⁶ The Lord raised up judges, who saved them from the power of their marauders, ¹⁷ but they did not listen to their judges. Instead, they prostituted themselves with other gods, bowing down to them. They quickly turned from the way of their ancestors, who had walked in obedience to the Lord's commands. They did not do as their ancestors did. ¹⁸ Whenever the Lord raised up a judge for the Israelites, the Lord was with him and saved the people from the power of their enemies while the judge was still alive. The Lord was moved to pity whenever they groaned because of those who were oppressing and afflicting them. ¹⁹ Whenever the judge died, the Israelites would act even more corruptly than their ancestors, following other gods to serve them and bow in worship to them. They did not turn from their evil practices or their obstinate ways.

²⁰ The Lord's anger burned against Israel, and he declared, "Because this nation has violated my covenant that I made with their ancestors and disobeyed me, ²¹ I will no longer drive out before them any of the nations Joshua left when he died. ²² I did this to test Israel and to see whether or not they would keep the Lord's way by walking in it, as their ancestors had." ²³ The Lord left these nations and did not drive them out immediately. He did not hand them over to Joshua.

◗ GOING DEEPER

DEUTERONOMY 4:1–10, 25–31
Call to Obedience

¹ Now, Israel, listen to the statutes and ordinances I am teaching you to follow, so that you may live, enter, and take possession of the land the Lord, the God of your ancestors, is giving you. ² You must not add anything to what I command you or take anything away from it, so that you may keep the commands of the Lord your God I am giving you. ³ Your eyes have seen what the Lord did at Baal-peor, for the Lord your God destroyed every one of you who followed Baal of Peor. ⁴ But you who have remained faithful to the Lord your God are all alive today. ⁵ Look, I have taught you statutes and ordinances as the Lord my God has commanded me, so that you may follow them in the land you are entering to possess. ⁶ Carefully follow them, for this will show your wisdom and understanding in the eyes of the peoples. When they hear about all these statutes, they will say, "This great nation is indeed a wise and understanding people." ⁷ For what great nation is there that has a god near to it as the Lord our God is to us whenever we call to him? ⁸ And what great nation has righteous statutes and ordinances like this entire law I set before you today?

⁹ Only be on your guard and diligently watch yourselves, so that you don't forget the things your eyes have seen and so that they don't slip from your mind as long as you live. Teach them to your children and your grandchildren. ¹⁰ The day

you stood before the Lord your God at Horeb, the Lord said to me, "Assemble the people before me, and I will let them hear my words, so that they may learn to fear me all the days they live on the earth and may instruct their children."

…

²⁵ When you have children and grandchildren and have been in the land a long time, and if you act corruptly, make an idol in the form of anything, and do what is evil in the sight of the Lord your God, angering him, ²⁶ I call heaven and earth as witnesses against you today that you will quickly perish from the land you are about to cross the Jordan to possess. You will not live long there, but you will certainly be destroyed. ²⁷ The Lord will scatter you among the peoples, and you will be reduced to a few survivors among the nations where the Lord your God will drive you. ²⁸ There you will worship man-made gods of wood and stone, which cannot see, hear, eat, or smell.

²⁹ **But from there, you will search for the Lord your God, and you will find him when you seek him with all your heart and all your soul.**

³⁰ When you are in distress and all these things have happened to you, in the future you will return to the Lord your God and obey him. ³¹ He will not leave you, destroy you, or forget the covenant with your ancestors that he swore to them by oath, because the Lord your God is a compassionate God.

HEBREWS 10:23

Let us hold on to the confession of our hope without wavering, since he who promised is faithful.

THE CYCLE OF REBELLION

One of the literary features in the book of Judges is a repeated cycle of rebellion, summarized in Judges 2:18–19:

"Whenever the LORD raised up a judge for the Israelites, the LORD was with him and saved the people from the power of their enemies while the judge was still alive. The LORD was moved to pity whenever they groaned because of those who were oppressing and afflicting them. Whenever the judge died, the Israelites would act even more corruptly than their ancestors, following other gods to serve them and bow in worship to them. They did not turn from their evil practices or their obstinate ways."

Most of the examples in Judges follow this pattern in its entirety. Toward the end of the book, the later stages of rescue and peace drop off, showing that this cycle is in a downward spiral.

This cycle of rebellion is not unique to Judges—we see it throughout Scripture. The only power that can break this cycle is the finished work of Jesus, who conquered the power of sin by accomplishing our salvation once and for all.

Therefore, there is now no condemnation for those in Christ Jesus, because the law of the Spirit of life in Christ Jesus has set you free from the law of sin and death.

ROMANS 8:1–2

OTHNIEL
Judges 3:7–11

- REBELLION
- OPPRESSION
- CRY FOR HELP
- RESCUE
- PEACE

EHUD
Judges 3:12–30

- REBELLION
- OPPRESSION
- CRY FOR HELP
- RESCUE
- PEACE

DEBORAH
Judges 4–5

- REBELLION
- OPPRESSION
- CRY FOR HELP
- RESCUE
- PEACE

GIDEON
Judges 6–8

- REBELLION
- OPPRESSION
- CRY FOR HELP
- RESCUE
- PEACE

JEPHTHAH
Judges 10:6–12:7

- REBELLION
- OPPRESSION
- CRY FOR HELP
- NO PEACE — RESCUE

SAMSON
Judges 13–16

- REBELLION
- OPPRESSION
- CRY FOR HELP
- NO PEACE — RESCUE

REBELLION Israel rebels against God.

OPPRESSION Israel becomes enslaved.

CRY FOR HELP Israel cries out to God.

RESCUE God raises up a judge to rescue Israel.

PEACE Israel is at peace.

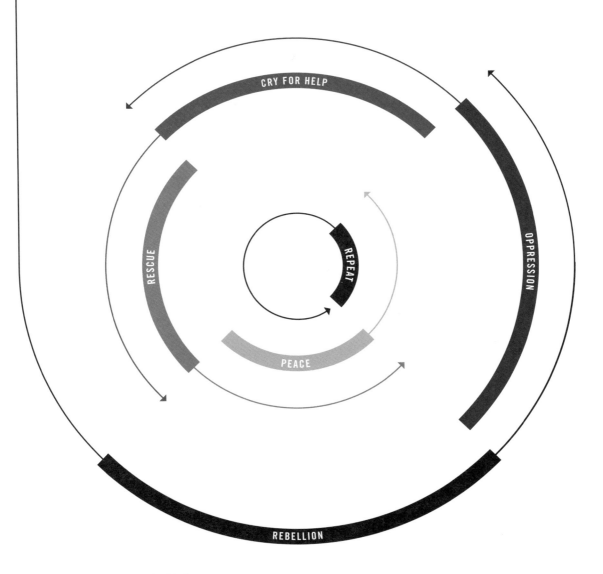

 Follow these cycles in greater detail in the margins of the daily readings.

THE LORD
TESTS ISRAEL

 This symbol marks an occurrence of the repeated cycle of rebellion. See page 26 for a full list.

OTHNIEL

Judges 3:7–11

REBELLION: 3:7
OPPRESSION: 3:8

CRY FOR HELP: 3:9
RESCUE: 3:9–10

PEACE: 3:11

JUDGES 3
The Lord Tests Israel

¹ These are the nations the LORD left in order to test all those in Israel who had experienced none of the wars in Canaan. ² This was to teach the future generations of the Israelites how to fight in battle, especially those who had not fought before. ³ These nations included the five rulers of the Philistines and all of the Canaanites, the Sidonians, and the Hivites who lived in the Lebanese mountains from Mount Baal-hermon as far as the entrance to Hamath. ⁴ The LORD left them to test Israel, to determine if they would keep the LORD's commands he had given their ancestors through Moses. ⁵ But they settled among the Canaanites, Hethites, Amorites, Perizzites, Hivites, and Jebusites. ⁶ The Israelites took their daughters as wives for themselves, gave their own daughters to their sons, and worshiped their gods.

Othniel, the First Judge

⁷ The Israelites did what was evil in the LORD's sight; they forgot the LORD their God and worshiped the Baals and the Asherahs. ⁸ The LORD's anger burned against Israel, and he sold them to King Cushan-rishathaim of Aram-naharaim, and the Israelites served him eight years.

⁹ The Israelites cried out to the LORD. So the LORD raised up Othniel son of Kenaz, Caleb's youngest brother, as a deliverer to save the Israelites. ¹⁰ The Spirit of the LORD came on him, and he judged Israel. Othniel went out to battle, and the LORD handed over King Cushan-rishathaim of Aram to him, so that Othniel overpowered him. ¹¹ Then the land had peace for forty years, and Othniel son of Kenaz died.

EHUD

Judges 3:12–30

REBELLION: 3:12
OPPRESSION: 3:12–14

CRY FOR HELP: 3:15
RESCUE: 3:15–29

Ehud

¹² The Israelites again did what was evil in the Lord's sight. He gave King Eglon of Moab power over Israel, because they had done what was evil in the Lord's sight. ¹³ After Eglon convinced the Ammonites and the Amalekites to join forces with him, he attacked and defeated Israel and took possession of the City of Palms. ¹⁴ The Israelites served King Eglon of Moab eighteen years.

¹⁵ Then the Israelites cried out to the Lord, and he raised up Ehud son of Gera, a left-handed Benjaminite, as a deliverer for them. The Israelites sent him with the tribute for King Eglon of Moab.

¹⁶ Ehud made himself a double-edged sword eighteen inches long. He strapped it to his right thigh under his clothes ¹⁷ and brought the tribute to King Eglon of Moab, who was an extremely fat man. ¹⁸ When Ehud had finished presenting the tribute, he dismissed the people who had carried it. ¹⁹ At the carved images near Gilgal he returned and said, "King Eglon, I have a secret message for you." The king said, "Silence!" and all his attendants left him. ²⁰ Then Ehud approached him while he was sitting alone in his upstairs room where it was cool. Ehud said, "I have a message from God for you," and the king stood up from his throne. ²¹ Ehud reached with his left hand, took the sword from his right thigh, and plunged it into Eglon's belly. ²² Even the handle went in after the blade, and Eglon's fat closed in over it, so that Ehud did not withdraw the sword from his belly. And the waste came out. ²³ Ehud escaped by way of the porch, closing and locking the doors of the upstairs room behind him.

²⁴ Ehud was gone when Eglon's servants came in. They looked and found the doors of the upstairs room locked and thought he was relieving himself in the cool room. ²⁵ The servants waited until they became embarrassed and saw that he had still not opened the doors of the upstairs room. So they took the key and opened the doors—and there was their lord lying dead on the floor!

²⁶ Ehud escaped while the servants waited. He passed the Jordan near the carved images and reached Seirah. ²⁷ After he arrived, he sounded the ram's horn throughout the hill country of Ephraim. The Israelites came down with him from the hill country, and he became their leader. ²⁸ He told them, "Follow me, because the Lord has handed over your enemies, the Moabites, to you." So they followed him, captured the fords of the Jordan leading to Moab, and did not allow anyone to cross over. ²⁹ At that time they struck down about ten thousand Moabites, all stout and able-bodied men. Not one of them escaped. ³⁰ Moab became subject to Israel that day, and the land had peace for eighty years.

PEACE: 3:30

Shamgar

[31] After Ehud, Shamgar son of Anath became judge. He also delivered Israel, striking down six hundred Philistines with a cattle prod.

◥ GOING DEEPER

DEUTERONOMY 8:1–2
Remember the Lord

[1] Carefully follow every command I am giving you today, so that you may live and increase, and may enter and take possession of the land the LORD swore to your ancestors.

[2] Remember that the LORD your God led you on the entire journey these forty years in the wilderness, so that he might humble you and test you to know what was in your heart,

whether or not you would keep his commands.

EPHESIANS 5:6–14

[6] Let no one deceive you with empty arguments, for God's wrath is coming on the disobedient because of these things. [7] Therefore, do not become their partners. [8] For you were once darkness, but now you are light in the Lord. Walk as children of light— [9] for the fruit of the light consists of all goodness, righteousness, and truth— [10] testing what is pleasing to the Lord. [11] Don't participate in the fruitless works of darkness, but instead expose them. [12] For it is shameful even to mention what is done by them in secret. [13] Everything exposed by the light is made visible, [14] for what makes everything visible is light. Therefore it is said:

Get up, sleeper, and rise up from the dead,
and Christ will shine on you.

DEBORAH
JUDGES ISRAEL

DEBORAH
Judges 4–5

REBELLION: 4:1
OPPRESSION: 4:2
CRY FOR HELP: 4:3

RESCUE: 4:4–5:31

JUDGES 4
Deborah and Barak

¹ The Israelites again did what was evil in the sight of the LORD after Ehud had died. ² So the LORD sold them to King Jabin of Canaan, who reigned in Hazor. The commander of his army was Sisera who lived in Harosheth of the Nations. ³ Then the Israelites cried out to the LORD, because Jabin had nine hundred iron chariots, and he harshly oppressed them twenty years.

⁴ Deborah, a prophetess and the wife of Lappidoth, was judging Israel at that time. ⁵ She would sit under the palm tree of Deborah between Ramah and Bethel in the hill country of Ephraim, and the Israelites went up to her to settle disputes.

⁶ She summoned Barak son of Abinoam from Kedesh in Naphtali and said to him, "Hasn't the LORD, the God of Israel, commanded you, 'Go, deploy the troops on Mount Tabor, and take with you ten thousand men from the Naphtalites and Zebulunites? ⁷ Then I will lure Sisera commander of Jabin's

army, his chariots, and his infantry at the Wadi Kishon to fight against you, and I will hand him over to you.'"

8 Barak said to her, "If you will go with me, I will go. But if you will not go with me, I will not go."

9 "I will gladly go with you," she said, "but you will receive no honor on the road you are about to take, because the LORD will sell Sisera to a woman." So Deborah got up and went with Barak to Kedesh. 10 Barak summoned Zebulun and Naphtali to Kedesh; ten thousand men followed him, and Deborah also went with him.

11 Now Heber the Kenite had moved away from the Kenites, the sons of Hobab, Moses's father-in-law, and pitched his tent beside the oak tree of Zaanannim, which was near Kedesh.

12 It was reported to Sisera that Barak son of Abinoam had gone up Mount Tabor. 13 Sisera summoned all his nine hundred iron chariots and all the troops who were with him from Harosheth of the Nations to the Wadi Kishon. 14 Then Deborah said to Barak, "Go! This is the day the LORD has handed Sisera over to you. Hasn't the LORD gone before you?" So Barak came down from Mount Tabor with ten thousand men following him.

15 The LORD threw Sisera, all his charioteers, and all his army into a panic before Barak's assault. Sisera left his chariot and fled on foot. 16 Barak pursued the chariots and the army as far as Harosheth of the Nations, and the whole army of Sisera fell by the sword; not a single man was left.

17 Meanwhile, Sisera had fled on foot to the tent of Jael, the wife of Heber the Kenite, because there was peace between King Jabin of Hazor and the family of Heber the Kenite. 18 Jael went out to greet Sisera and said to him, "Come in, my lord. Come in with me. Don't be afraid." So he went into her tent, and she covered him with a blanket. 19 He said to her, "Please give me a little water to drink for I am thirsty." She opened a container of milk, gave him a drink, and covered him again. 20 Then he said to her, "Stand at the entrance to the tent. If a man comes and asks you, 'Is there a man here?' say, 'No.'" 21 While he was sleeping from exhaustion, Heber's wife, Jael, took a tent peg, grabbed a hammer, and went silently to Sisera. She hammered the peg into his temple and drove it into the ground, and he died.

22 When Barak arrived in pursuit of Sisera, Jael went out to greet him and said to him, "Come and I will show you the man you are looking for." So he went in with her, and there was Sisera lying dead with a tent peg through his temple!

23 That day God subdued King Jabin of Canaan before the Israelites. 24 The power of the Israelites continued to increase against King Jabin of Canaan until they destroyed him.

JUDGES 5
Deborah's Song

1 On that day Deborah and Barak son of Abinoam sang:
2 When the leaders lead in Israel,
when the people volunteer,
blessed be the LORD.
3 Listen, kings! Pay attention, princes!
I will sing to the LORD;
I will sing praise to the LORD God of Israel.
4 LORD, when you came from Seir,
when you marched from the fields of Edom,
the earth trembled,
the skies poured rain,
and the clouds poured water.
5 The mountains melted before the LORD,
even Sinai, before the LORD, the God of Israel.

6 In the days of Shamgar son of Anath,
in the days of Jael,
the main roads were deserted
because travelers kept to the side roads.
7 Villages were deserted,
they were deserted in Israel,
until I, Deborah, arose,
a mother in Israel.
8 Israel chose new gods,
then there was war in the city gates.
Not a shield or spear was seen

among forty thousand in Israel.
⁹ My heart is with the leaders of Israel,
with the volunteers of the people.
Blessed be the LORD!
¹⁰ You who ride on white donkeys,
who sit on saddle blankets,
and who travel on the road, give praise!
¹¹ Let them tell the righteous acts of the LORD,
the righteous deeds of his villagers in Israel,
with the voices of the singers at the watering places.
Then the LORD's people went down to the city gates.
¹² "Awake! Awake, Deborah!
Awake! Awake, sing a song!
Arise, Barak,
and take your prisoners,
son of Abinoam!"
¹³ Then the survivors came down to the nobles;
the LORD's people came down to me against the warriors.
¹⁴ Those with their roots in Amalek came from Ephraim;
Benjamin came with your people after you.
The leaders came down from Machir,
and those who carry a marshal's staff came from Zebulun.
¹⁵ The princes of Issachar were with Deborah;
Issachar was with Barak;
they were under his leadership in the valley.
There was great searching of heart
among the clans of Reuben.
¹⁶ Why did you sit among the sheep pens
listening to the playing of pipes for the flocks?
There was great searching of heart
among the clans of Reuben.
¹⁷ Gilead remained beyond the Jordan.
Dan, why did you linger at the ships?
Asher remained at the seashore
and stayed in his harbors.
¹⁸ The people of Zebulun defied death,
Naphtali also, on the heights of the battlefield.

¹⁹ Kings came and fought.
Then the kings of Canaan fought
at Taanach by the Waters of Megiddo,
but they did not plunder the silver.

²⁰ The stars fought from the heavens;
the stars fought with Sisera from their paths.
²¹ The river Kishon swept them away,
the ancient river, the river Kishon.
March on, my soul, in strength!
²² The horses' hooves then hammered—
the galloping, galloping of his stallions.
²³ "Curse Meroz," says the angel of the LORD,
"Bitterly curse her inhabitants,
for they did not come to help the LORD,
to help the LORD with the warriors."

²⁴ Most blessed of women is Jael,
the wife of Heber the Kenite;
she is most blessed among tent-dwelling women.
²⁵ He asked for water; she gave him milk.
She brought him cream in a majestic bowl.
²⁶ She reached for a tent peg,
her right hand, for a workman's hammer.
Then she hammered Sisera—
she crushed his head;
she shattered and pierced his temple.
²⁷ He collapsed, he fell, he lay down between her feet;
he collapsed, he fell between her feet;
where he collapsed, there he fell—dead.

²⁸ Sisera's mother looked through the window;
she peered through the lattice, crying out:
"Why is his chariot so long in coming?
Why don't I hear the hoofbeats of his horses?"
²⁹ Her wisest princesses answer her;
she even answers herself:
³⁰ "Are they not finding and dividing the spoil—
a girl or two for each warrior,
the spoil of colored garments for Sisera,
the spoil of an embroidered garment or two for my neck?"

³¹ LORD, may all your enemies perish as Sisera did.
But may those who love him
be like the rising of the sun in its strength.

PEACE: 5:31   And the land had peace for forty years.

ZEPHANIAH 3:14–17

[14] Sing for joy, Daughter Zion;
shout loudly, Israel!
Be glad and celebrate with all your heart,
Daughter Jerusalem!

[15] The LORD has removed your punishment;

he has turned back your enemy.
The King of Israel, the LORD, is among you;
you need no longer fear harm.
[16] On that day it will be said to Jerusalem:
"Do not fear;
Zion, do not let your hands grow weak.
[17] The LORD your God is among you,
a warrior who saves.
He will rejoice over you with gladness.
He will be quiet in his love.
He will delight in you with singing."

LUKE 1:68–75

[68] Blessed is the Lord, the God of Israel,
because he has visited
and provided redemption for his people.
[69] He has raised up a horn of salvation for us
in the house of his servant David,
[70] just as he spoke by the mouth
of his holy prophets in ancient times;
[71] salvation from our enemies
and from the hand of those who hate us.
[72] He has dealt mercifully with our ancestors
and remembered his holy covenant—
[73] the oath that he swore to our father Abraham,
to grant that we,
[74] having been rescued
from the hand of our enemies,
would serve him without fear
[75] in holiness and righteousness
in his presence all our days.

THE LORD CALLS GIDEON

GIDEON
Judges 6–8

REBELLION: 6:1
OPPRESSION: 6:1–5

CRY FOR HELP: 6:6–7

RESCUE: 6:8–8:21

JUDGES 6

Midian Oppresses Israel

¹ The Israelites did what was evil in the sight of the Lord. So the Lord handed them over to Midian seven years, ² and they oppressed Israel. Because of Midian, the Israelites made hiding places for themselves in the mountains, caves, and strongholds. ³ Whenever the Israelites planted crops, the Midianites, Amalekites, and the people of the east came and attacked them. ⁴ They encamped against them and destroyed the produce of the land, even as far as Gaza. They left nothing for Israel to eat, as well as no sheep, ox, or donkey. ⁵ For the Midianites came with their cattle and their tents like a great swarm of locusts. They and their camels were without number, and they entered the land to lay waste to it. ⁶ So Israel became poverty-stricken because of Midian, and the Israelites cried out to the Lord.

⁷ When the Israelites cried out to him because of Midian, ⁸ the Lord sent a prophet to them. He said to them, "This is what the Lord God of Israel says: 'I brought you out of Egypt and out of the place of slavery. ⁹ I rescued you from the power of Egypt and the power of all who oppressed you. I drove them out before you and gave you their land. ¹⁰ I said to you: I am the Lord your God. Do not fear the gods of the Amorites whose land you live in. But you did not obey me.'"

The Lord Calls Gideon

¹¹ The angel of the Lord came, and he sat under the oak that was in Ophrah, which belonged to Joash, the Abiezrite. His son Gideon was threshing wheat in the winepress in order to hide it from the Midianites. ¹² Then the angel of

the LORD appeared to him and said, "The LORD is with you, valiant warrior."

¹³ Gideon said to him, "Please, my lord, if the LORD is with us, why has all this happened? And where are all his wonders that our ancestors told us about? They said, 'Hasn't the LORD brought us out of Egypt?' But now the LORD has abandoned us and handed us over to Midian."

¹⁴ The LORD turned to him and said, "Go in the strength you have and deliver Israel from the grasp of Midian. I am sending you!"

¹⁵ He said to him, "Please, Lord, how can I deliver Israel? Look, my family is the weakest in Manasseh, and I am the youngest in my father's family."

¹⁶ "But I will be with you," the LORD said to him. "You will strike Midian down as if it were one man."

¹⁷ Then he said to him, "If I have found favor with you, give me a sign that you are speaking with me. ¹⁸ Please do not leave this place until I return to you. Let me bring my gift and set it before you."

And he said, "I will stay until you return."

¹⁹ So Gideon went and prepared a young goat and unleavened bread from a half bushel of flour. He placed the meat in a basket and the broth in a pot. He brought them out and offered them to him under the oak.

²⁰ The angel of God said to him, "Take the meat with the unleavened bread, put it on this stone, and pour the broth on it." So he did that.

²¹ The angel of the LORD extended the tip of the staff that was in his hand and touched the meat and the unleavened bread. Fire came up from the rock and consumed the meat and the unleavened bread. Then the angel of the LORD vanished from his sight.

²² When Gideon realized that he was the angel of the LORD, he said, "Oh no, Lord GOD! I have seen the angel of the LORD face to face!"

²³ But the LORD said to him, "Peace to you. Don't be afraid, for you will not die." ²⁴ So Gideon built an altar to the LORD there and called it The LORD Is Peace. It is still in Ophrah of the Abiezrites today.

Gideon Tears Down a Baal Altar

²⁵ On that very night the LORD said to him, "Take your father's young bull and a second bull seven years old. Then tear down the altar of Baal that belongs to your father and cut down the Asherah pole beside it. ²⁶ Build a well-constructed altar to the LORD your God on the top of this mound. Take the second bull and offer it as a burnt offering with the wood of the Asherah pole you cut down." ²⁷ So Gideon took ten of his male servants and did as the LORD had told him. But because he was too afraid of his father's family and the men of the city to do it in the daytime, he did it at night.

²⁸ When the men of the city got up in the morning, they found Baal's altar torn down, the Asherah pole beside it cut down, and the second bull offered up on the altar that had been built. ²⁹ They said to each other, "Who did this?" After they made a thorough investigation, they said, "Gideon son of Joash did it."

³⁰ Then the men of the city said to Joash, "Bring out your son. He must die, because he tore down Baal's altar and cut down the Asherah pole beside it."

³¹ But Joash said to all who stood against him, "Would you plead Baal's case for him? Would you save him? Whoever pleads his case will be put to death by morning! If he is a god, let him plead his own case because someone tore down his altar."

³² That day Gideon was called Jerubbaal, since Joash said, "Let Baal contend with him," because he tore down his altar.

The Sign of the Fleece

³³ All the Midianites, Amalekites, and people of the east gathered together, crossed over the Jordan, and camped in the Jezreel Valley.

³⁴ The Spirit of the LORD enveloped Gideon, and he blew the ram's horn and the Abiezrites rallied behind him. ³⁵ He sent messengers throughout all of Manasseh, who rallied behind him. He also sent messengers throughout Asher, Zebulun, and Naphtali, who also came to meet him.

³⁶ Then Gideon said to God, "If you will deliver Israel by me, as you said, ³⁷ I will put a wool fleece here on the threshing floor. If dew is only on the fleece, and all the ground is dry, I will know that you will deliver Israel by me, as you said." ³⁸ And that is what happened. When he got up early in the morning, he squeezed the fleece and wrung dew out of it, filling a bowl with water.

³⁹ Gideon then said to God, "Don't be angry with me; let me speak one more time. Please allow me to make one more test with the fleece. Let it remain dry, and the dew be all over the ground." ⁴⁰ That night God did as Gideon requested: only the fleece was dry, and dew was all over the ground.

♥ GOING DEEPER

ISAIAH 25:1–9
Salvation and Judgment on That Day

¹ LORD, you are my God;
I will exalt you. I will praise your name,
for you have accomplished wonders,
plans formed long ago, with perfect faithfulness.
² For you have turned the city into a pile of rocks,
a fortified city, into ruins;

the fortress of barbarians is no longer a city;
it will never be rebuilt.
³ Therefore, a strong people will honor you.
The cities of violent nations will fear you.
⁴ For you have been a stronghold for the poor person,
a stronghold for the needy in his distress,
a refuge from storms and a shade from heat.
When the breath of the violent
is like a storm against a wall,
⁵ like heat in a dry land,
you will subdue the uproar of barbarians.
As the shade of a cloud cools the heat of the day,
so he will silence the song of the violent.

⁶ On this mountain,
the LORD of Armies will prepare for all the peoples a feast
   of choice meat,
a feast with aged wine, prime cuts of choice meat,
   fine vintage wine.
⁷ On this mountain
he will swallow up the burial shroud,
the shroud over all the peoples,
the sheet covering all the nations.

⁸ When he has swallowed up
   death once and for all,
the Lord GOD will wipe away the tears
from every face

and remove his people's disgrace
from the whole earth,
for the LORD has spoken.

⁹ On that day it will be said,
"Look, this is our God;
we have waited for him, and he has saved us.
This is the LORD; we have waited for him.
Let's rejoice and be glad in his salvation."

GRACE DAY

Take this day to catch up on your reading, pray, and rest in the presence of the Lord.

Each Saturday we'll turn from the tragedy of Judges to the hope of the gospel in Psalm 32, a psalm about joy and forgiveness.

PSALM 32:1–2

How joyful is the one
whose transgression is forgiven,
whose sin is covered!
How joyful is a person whom
the Lᴏʀᴅ does not charge with iniquity
and in whose spirit is no deceit!

Scripture is God-breathed and true. When we memorize it,
we carry His Word with us wherever we go.

As we read, we will memorize Judges 2:11–12a, verses that
illustrate the repeating cycle of sin seen in the book of Judges.

We'll start by memorizing part of verse 11.

[11] The Israelites did what was evil in the LORD's sight. They worshiped the Baals [12] and abandoned the LORD, the God of their ancestors, who had brought them out of Egypt.

See tips for memorizing Scripture on page 124.

GIDEON'S ARMY

JUDGES 7
God Selects Gideon's Army

¹ Jerubbaal (that is, Gideon) and all the troops who were with him, got up early and camped beside the spring of Harod. The camp of Midian was north of them, below the hill of Moreh, in the valley. ² The Lord said to Gideon, "You have too many troops for me to hand the Midianites over to them, or else Israel might elevate themselves over me and say, 'I saved myself.' ³ Now announce to the troops, 'Whoever is fearful and trembling may turn back and leave Mount Gilead.'" So twenty-two thousand of the troops turned back, but ten thousand remained.

⁴ Then the Lord said to Gideon, "There are still too many troops. Take them down to the water, and I will test them for you there. If I say to you, 'This one can go with you,' he can go. But if I say about anyone, 'This one cannot go with you,' he cannot go." ⁵ So he brought the troops down to the water, and the Lord said to Gideon, "Separate everyone who laps water with his tongue like a dog. Do the same with everyone who kneels to drink." ⁶ The number of those who lapped with their hands to their mouths was three hundred men, and all the rest of the troops knelt to drink water. ⁷ The Lord said to Gideon, "I will deliver you with the three hundred men who lapped and hand the Midianites over to you. But everyone else is to go home." ⁸ So Gideon sent all the Israelites to their tents but kept the three hundred troops, who took the provisions and their rams' horns. The camp of Midian was below him in the valley.

Gideon Spies on the Midianite Camp

[9] That night the LORD said to him, "Get up and attack the camp, for I have handed it over to you. [10] But if you are afraid to attack the camp, go down with Purah your servant. [11] Listen to what they say, and then you will be encouraged to attack the camp." So he went down with Purah his servant to the outpost of the troops who were in the camp.

[12] Now the Midianites, Amalekites, and all the people of the east had settled down in the valley like a swarm of locusts, and their camels were as innumerable as the sand on the seashore. [13] When Gideon arrived, there was a man telling his friend about a dream. He said, "Listen, I had a dream: a loaf of barley bread came tumbling into the Midianite camp, struck a tent, and it fell. The loaf turned the tent upside down so that it collapsed."

[14] His friend answered, "This is nothing less than the sword of Gideon son of Joash, the Israelite. God has handed the entire Midianite camp over to him."

Gideon Attacks the Midianites

[15] When Gideon heard the account of the dream and its interpretation, he bowed in worship. He returned to Israel's camp and said, "Get up, for the LORD has handed the Midianite camp over to you." [16] Then he divided the three hundred men into three companies and gave each of the men a ram's horn in one hand and an empty pitcher with a torch inside it in the other hand.

[17] "Watch me," he said to them, "and do what I do. When I come to the outpost of the camp, do as I do. [18] When I and everyone with me blow our rams' horns, you are also to blow your rams' horns all around the camp. Then you will say, 'For the LORD and for Gideon!'"

[19] Gideon and the hundred men who were with him went to the outpost of the camp at the beginning of the middle watch after the sentries had been stationed. They blew their rams' horns and broke the pitchers that were in their hands. [20] The three companies blew their rams' horns and shattered their pitchers. They held their torches in their left hands and their rams' horns to blow in their right hands, and they shouted, "A sword for the LORD and for Gideon!" [21] Each Israelite took his position around the camp, and the entire Midianite army began to run, and they cried out as they fled. [22] When Gideon's men blew their three hundred rams' horns, the LORD caused the men in the whole army to turn on each other with their swords. They fled to Acacia House in the direction of Zererah as far as the border of Abel-meholah near Tabbath. [23] Then the men of Israel were called from Naphtali, Asher, and Manasseh, and they pursued the Midianites.

The Men of Ephraim Join the Battle

[24] Gideon sent messengers throughout the hill country of Ephraim with this message: "Come down to intercept the Midianites and take control of the watercourses ahead of them as far as Beth-barah and the Jordan." So all the men of Ephraim were called out, and they took control of the watercourses as far as Beth-barah and the Jordan. [25] They captured Oreb and Zeeb, the two princes of Midian; they killed Oreb at the rock of Oreb and Zeeb at the winepress of Zeeb, while they were pursuing the Midianites. They brought the heads of Oreb and Zeeb to Gideon across the Jordan.

◼ GOING DEEPER

ISAIAH 41:10

"Do not fear, for I am with you;

do not be afraid, for I am your God.
I will strengthen you; I will help you;
I will hold on to you with my righteous
  right hand."

EPHESIANS 6:10

Finally, be strengthened by the Lord and by his vast strength.

NOTES

GIDEON'S LEGACY

JUDGES 8

¹ The men of Ephraim said to him, "Why have you done this to us, not calling us when you went to fight against the Midianites?" And they argued with him violently.

² So he said to them, "What have I done now compared to you? Is not the gleaning of Ephraim better than the grape harvest of Abiezer? ³ God handed over to you Oreb and Zeeb, the two princes of Midian. What was I able to do compared to you?" When he said this, their anger against him subsided.

Gideon Pursues the Kings of Midian

⁴ Gideon and the three hundred men came to the Jordan and crossed it. They were exhausted but still in pursuit. ⁵ He said to the men of Succoth, "Please give some loaves of bread to the troops under my command, because they are exhausted, for I am pursuing Zebah and Zalmunna, the kings of Midian."

⁶ But the princes of Succoth asked, "Are Zebah and Zalmunna now in your hands that we should give bread to your army?"

⁷ Gideon replied, "Very well, when the Lord has handed Zebah and Zalmunna over to me, I will tear your flesh with

thorns and briers from the wilderness!" [8] He went from there to Penuel and asked the same thing from them. The men of Penuel answered just as the men of Succoth had answered. [9] He also told the men of Penuel, "When I return safely, I will tear down this tower!"

[10] Now Zebah and Zalmunna were in Karkor, and with them was their army of about fifteen thousand men, who were all those left of the entire army of the people of the east. Those who had been killed were one hundred twenty thousand armed men. [11] Gideon traveled on the caravan route east of Nobah and Jogbehah and attacked their army while the army felt secure. [12] Zebah and Zalmunna fled, and he pursued them. He captured these two kings of Midian and routed the entire army.

[13] Gideon son of Joash returned from the battle by the Ascent of Heres. [14] He captured a youth from the men of Succoth and interrogated him. The youth wrote down for him the names of the seventy-seven leaders and elders of Succoth. [15] Then he went to the men of Succoth and said, "Here are Zebah and Zalmunna. You taunted me about them, saying, 'Are Zebah and Zalmunna now in your power that we should give bread to your exhausted men?'" [16] So he took the elders of the city, and he took some thorns and briers from the wilderness, and he disciplined the men of Succoth with them. [17] He also tore down the tower of Penuel and killed the men of the city.

[18] He asked Zebah and Zalmunna, "What kind of men did you kill at Tabor?"

"They were like you," they said. "Each resembled the son of a king."

[19] So he said, "They were my brothers, the sons of my mother! As the Lord lives, if you had let them live, I would not kill you." [20] Then he said to Jether, his firstborn, "Get up and kill them." The youth did not draw his sword, for he was afraid because he was still a youth.

[21] Zebah and Zalmunna said, "Get up and strike us down yourself, for a man is judged by his strength." So Gideon got up, killed Zebah and Zalmunna, and took the crescent ornaments that were on the necks of their camels.

Gideon's Legacy

[22] Then the Israelites said to Gideon, "Rule over us, you as well as your sons and your grandsons, for you delivered us from the power of Midian."

[23] But Gideon said to them, "I will not rule over you, and my son will not rule over you; the Lord will rule over you." [24] Then he said to them, "Let me make a request of you: Everyone give me an earring from his plunder." Now the enemy had gold earrings because they were Ishmaelites.

25 They said, "We agree to give them." So they spread out a cloak, and everyone threw an earring from his plunder on it. 26 The weight of the gold earrings he requested was forty-three pounds of gold, in addition to the crescent ornaments and ear pendants, the purple garments on the kings of Midian, and the chains on the necks of their camels. 27 Gideon made an ephod from all this and put it in Ophrah, his hometown. Then all Israel prostituted themselves by worshiping it there, and it became a snare to Gideon and his household.

28 So Midian was subdued before the Israelites, and they were no longer a threat. The land had peace for forty years during the days of Gideon. 29 Jerubbaal (that is, Gideon) son of Joash went back to live at his house.

30 Gideon had seventy sons, his own offspring, since he had many wives. 31 His concubine who was in Shechem also bore him a son, and he named him Abimelech. 32 Then Gideon son of Joash died at a good old age and was buried in the tomb of his father Joash in Ophrah of the Abiezrites.

33 When Gideon died, the Israelites turned and prostituted themselves by worshiping the Baals and made Baal-berith their god. 34 The Israelites did not remember the LORD their God who had rescued them from the hand of the enemies around them. 35 They did not show kindness to the house of Jerubbaal (that is, Gideon) for all the good he had done for Israel.

🔖 GOING DEEPER

ZECHARIAH 10:6

"I will strengthen the house of Judah
and deliver the house of Joseph.

I will restore them
because I have compassion on them,

and they will be
as though I had never rejected them.
For I am the LORD their God,
and I will answer them."

1 CORINTHIANS 1:24–31

[24] Yet to those who are called, both Jews and Greeks, Christ is the power of God and the wisdom of God, [25] because God's foolishness is wiser than human wisdom, and God's weakness is stronger than human strength.

Boasting Only in the Lord

[26] Brothers and sisters, consider your calling: Not many were wise from a human perspective, not many powerful, not many of noble birth. [27] Instead, God has chosen what is foolish in the world to shame the wise, and God has chosen what is weak in the world to shame the strong. [28] God has chosen what is insignificant and despised in the world—what is viewed as nothing—to bring to nothing what is viewed as something, [29] so that no one may boast in his presence. [30] It is from him that you are in Christ Jesus, who became wisdom from God for us—our righteousness, sanctification, and redemption— [31] in order that, as it is written: Let the one who boasts, boast in the Lord.

ABIMELECH BECOMES KING

JUDGES 9

Abimelech Becomes King

¹ Abimelech son of Jerubbaal went to Shechem and spoke to his uncles and to his mother's whole clan, saying, ² "Please speak in the hearing of all the citizens of Shechem, 'Is it better for you that seventy men, all the sons of Jerubbaal, rule over you or that one man rule over you?' Remember that I am your own flesh and blood."

³ His mother's relatives spoke all these words about him in the hearing of all the citizens of Shechem, and they were favorable to Abimelech, for they said, "He is our brother." ⁴ So they gave him seventy pieces of silver from the temple of Baal-berith. Abimelech used it to hire worthless and reckless men, and they followed him. ⁵ He went to his father's house in Ophrah and killed his seventy brothers, the sons of Jerubbaal, on top of a large stone. But Jotham, the youngest son of Jerubbaal, survived, because he hid. ⁶ Then all the citizens of Shechem and of Beth-millo gathered together and proceeded to make Abimelech king at the oak of the pillar in Shechem.

Jotham's Parable

⁷ When they told Jotham, he climbed to the top of Mount Gerizim, raised his voice, and called to them:

Listen to me, citizens of Shechem,
and may God listen to you:

⁸ The trees decided
to anoint a king over themselves.
They said to the olive tree, "Reign over us."
⁹ But the olive tree said to them,
"Should I stop giving my oil
that people use to honor both God and men,
and rule over the trees?"

¹⁰ Then the trees said to the fig tree,
"Come and reign over us."
¹¹ But the fig tree said to them,
"Should I stop giving
my sweetness and my good fruit,
and rule over trees?"

¹² Later, the trees said to the grapevine,
"Come and reign over us."
¹³ But the grapevine said to them,
"Should I stop giving my wine
that cheers both God and man,
and rule over trees?"

¹⁴ Finally, all the trees said to the bramble,
"Come and reign over us."
¹⁵ The bramble said to the trees,
"If you really are anointing me
as king over you,
come and find refuge in my shade.
But if not,
may fire come out from the bramble
and consume the cedars of Lebanon."

¹⁶ "Now if you have acted faithfully and honestly in making Abimelech king, if you have done well by Jerubbaal and his family, and if you have rewarded him appropriately for what he did— ¹⁷ for my father fought for you, risked his life, and rescued you from Midian, ¹⁸ and now you have attacked my father's family today, killed his seventy sons on top of a large stone, and made Abimelech, the son of his slave woman, king over the citizens of Shechem 'because he is your brother'— ¹⁹ so if you have acted faithfully and honestly with Jerubbaal and his house this day, rejoice in Abimelech and may he also rejoice in you. ²⁰ But if not, may fire come from Abimelech and consume the citizens of Shechem and Beth-millo, and may fire come from the citizens of Shechem and Beth-millo and consume Abimelech." ²¹ Then Jotham fled, escaping to Beer, and lived there because of his brother Abimelech.

Abimelech's Punishment

²² When Abimelech had ruled over Israel three years, ²³ God sent an evil spirit between Abimelech and the citizens of Shechem. They treated Abimelech deceitfully, ²⁴ so that the crime against the seventy sons of Jerubbaal might come to justice and their blood would be avenged on their brother Abimelech, who killed them, and on the citizens of Shechem, who had helped him kill his brothers. ²⁵ The citizens of Shechem rebelled against him by putting men in ambush on the tops of the mountains, and they robbed everyone who passed by them on the road. So this was reported to Abimelech.

²⁶ Gaal son of Ebed came with his brothers and crossed into Shechem, and the citizens of Shechem trusted him. ²⁷ So they went out to the countryside and harvested grapes from their vineyards. They trampled the grapes and held a celebration. Then they went to the house of their god, and as they ate and drank, they cursed Abimelech. ²⁸ Gaal son of Ebed said, "Who is Abimelech and who is Shechem that we should serve him? Isn't he the son of Jerubbaal, and isn't Zebul his officer? You are to serve the men of Hamor, the father of Shechem. Why should we serve Abimelech? ²⁹ If only these people were in my power, I would remove Abimelech." So he said to Abimelech, "Gather your army and come out."

³⁰ When Zebul, the ruler of the city, heard the words of Gaal son of Ebed, he was angry. ³¹ So he secretly sent messengers to Abimelech, saying, "Beware! Gaal son of Ebed and his brothers have come to Shechem and are turning the city against you. ³² Now tonight, you and the troops with you, come and wait in ambush in the countryside. ³³ Then get

up early, and at sunrise attack the city. When he and the troops who are with him come out against you, do to him whatever you can." ³⁴ So Abimelech and all the troops with him got up at night and waited in ambush for Shechem in four units.

³⁵ Gaal son of Ebed went out and stood at the entrance of the city gate. Then Abimelech and the troops who were with him got up from their ambush. ³⁶ When Gaal saw the troops, he said to Zebul, "Look, troops are coming down from the mountaintops!" But Zebul said to him, "The shadows of the mountains look like men to you."

³⁷ Then Gaal spoke again, "Look, troops are coming down from the central part of the land, and one unit is coming from the direction of the Diviners' Oak." ³⁸ Zebul replied, "What do you have to say now? You said, 'Who is Abimelech that we should serve him?' Aren't these the troops you despised? Now go and fight them!"

³⁹ So Gaal went out leading the citizens of Shechem and fought against Abimelech, ⁴⁰ but Abimelech pursued him, and Gaal fled before him. Numerous bodies were strewn as far as the entrance of the city gate. ⁴¹ Abimelech stayed in Arumah, and Zebul drove Gaal and his brothers from Shechem.

⁴² The next day when the people of Shechem went into the countryside, this was reported to Abimelech. ⁴³ He took the troops, divided them into three companies, and waited in ambush in the countryside. He looked, and the people were coming out of the city, so he arose against them and struck them down. ⁴⁴ Then Abimelech and the units that were with him rushed forward and took their stand at the entrance of the city gate. The other two units rushed against all who were in the countryside and struck them down. ⁴⁵ So Abimelech fought against the city that entire day, captured it, and killed the people who were in it. Then he tore down the city and sowed it with salt.

⁴⁶ When all the citizens of the Tower of Shechem heard, they entered the inner chamber of the temple of El-berith. ⁴⁷ Then it was reported to Abimelech that all the citizens of the Tower of Shechem had gathered. ⁴⁸ So Abimelech and all the troops who were with him went up to Mount Zalmon. Abimelech took his ax in his hand and cut a branch from the trees. He picked up the branch, put it on his shoulder, and said to the troops who were with him, "Hurry and do what you have seen me do." ⁴⁹ Each of the troops also cut his own branch and followed Abimelech. They put the branches against the inner chamber and set it on fire; about a thousand men and women died, including all the men of the Tower of Shechem.

⁵⁰ Abimelech went to Thebez, camped against it, and captured it. ⁵¹ There was a strong tower inside the city, and all the men, women, and citizens of the city

fled there. They locked themselves in and went up to the roof of the tower. [52] When Abimelech came to attack the tower, he approached its entrance to set it on fire. [53] But a woman threw the upper portion of a millstone on Abimelech's head and fractured his skull. [54] He quickly called his armor-bearer and said to him, "Draw your sword and kill me, or they'll say about me, 'A woman killed him.'" So his armor-bearer ran him through, and he died. [55] When the Israelites saw that Abimelech was dead, they all went home.

[56] In this way, God brought back Abimelech's evil—the evil that Abimelech had done to his father when he killed his seventy brothers. [57] God also brought back to the men of Shechem all their evil. So the curse of Jotham son of Jerubbaal came upon them.

♥ GOING DEEPER

PSALM 68:19–21

[19] Blessed be the Lord!
Day after day he bears our burdens;
God is our salvation.   *Selah*
[20] Our God is a God of salvation,
and escape from death belongs to the LORD my Lord.
[21] Surely God crushes the heads of his enemies,
the hairy brow of one who goes on in his guilty acts.

MATTHEW 7:15–20

[15] "Be on your guard against false prophets who come to you in sheep's clothing but inwardly are ravaging wolves.

[16] You'll recognize them by their fruit. Are grapes gathered from thornbushes or figs from thistles? [17] In the same way, every good tree produces good fruit, but a bad tree produces bad fruit. [18] A good tree can't produce bad fruit; neither can a bad tree produce good fruit. [19] Every tree that doesn't produce good fruit is cut down and thrown into the fire. [20] So you'll recognize them by their fruit."

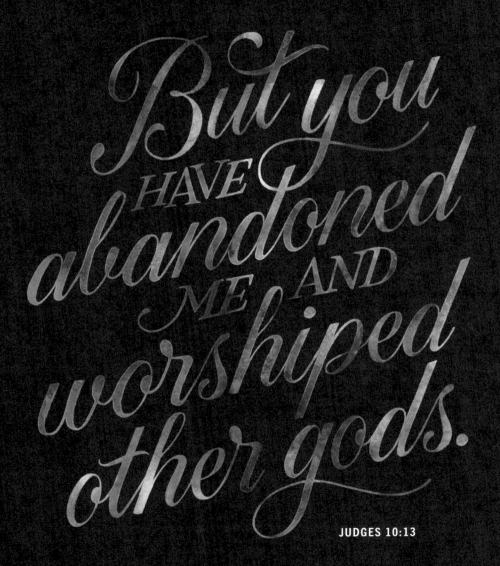

But you have abandoned me and worshiped other gods.

JUDGES 10:13

ISRAEL'S REBELLION AND REPENTANCE

 JEPHTHAH
Judges 10:6–12:7

REBELLION: 10:6
OPPRESSION: 10:7–9

CRY FOR HELP: 10:10–16

JUDGES 10

Tola and Jair

¹ After Abimelech, Tola son of Puah, son of Dodo became judge and began to deliver Israel. He was from Issachar and lived in Shamir in the hill country of Ephraim. ² Tola judged Israel twenty-three years and when he died, was buried in Shamir.

³ After him came Jair the Gileadite, who judged Israel twenty-two years. ⁴ He had thirty sons who rode on thirty donkeys. They had thirty towns in Gilead, which are still called Jair's Villages today. ⁵ When Jair died, he was buried in Kamon.

Israel's Rebellion and Repentance

⁶ Then the Israelites again did what was evil in the sight of the LORD. They worshiped the Baals and the Ashtoreths, the gods of Aram, Sidon, and Moab, and the gods of the Ammonites and the Philistines. They abandoned the LORD and did not worship him. ⁷ So the LORD's anger burned against Israel, and he sold them to the Philistines and the Ammonites. ⁸ They shattered and crushed the Israelites that year, and for eighteen years they did the same to all the Israelites who were on the other side of the Jordan in the land of the Amorites in Gilead. ⁹ The Ammonites also crossed the Jordan to fight against Judah, Benjamin, and the house of Ephraim. Israel was greatly oppressed, ¹⁰ so they cried out to the LORD, saying, "We have sinned against you. We have abandoned our God and worshiped the Baals."

[11] The Lord said to the Israelites, "When the Egyptians, Amorites, Ammonites, Philistines, [12] Sidonians, Amalekites, and Maonites oppressed you, and you cried out to me, did I not deliver you from them? [13] But you have abandoned me and worshiped other gods. Therefore, I will not deliver you again. [14] Go and cry out to the gods you have chosen. Let them deliver you whenever you are oppressed."

[15] But the Israelites said, "We have sinned. Deal with us as you see fit; only rescue us today!" [16] So they got rid of the foreign gods among them and worshiped the Lord, and he became weary of Israel's misery.

[17] The Ammonites were called together, and they camped in Gilead. So the Israelites assembled and camped at Mizpah. [18] The rulers of Gilead said to one another, "Which man will begin the fight against the Ammonites? He will be the leader of all the inhabitants of Gilead."

◆ GOING DEEPER

ISAIAH 30:15–18

[15] For the Lord God, the Holy One of Israel, has said:
"You will be delivered by returning and resting;
your strength will lie in quiet confidence.
But you are not willing."
[16] You say, "No!
We will escape on horses"—
therefore you will escape!—
and, "We will ride on fast horses"—
but those who pursue you will be faster.
[17] One thousand will flee at the threat of one,
at the threat of five you will flee,
until you remain
like a solitary pole on a mountaintop
or a banner on a hill.

The Lord's Mercy to Israel

[18] Therefore the Lord is waiting to
show you mercy,
and is rising up to show
you compassion,
for the Lord is a just God.
All who wait patiently for him
are happy.

2 CORINTHIANS 7:9–12

[9] I now rejoice, not because you were grieved, but because your grief led to repentance. For you were grieved as God willed, so that you didn't experience any loss from us. [10] For godly grief produces a repentance that leads to salvation without regret, but worldly grief produces death. [11] For consider how much diligence this very thing—this grieving as God wills—has produced in you: what a desire to clear yourselves, what indignation, what fear, what deep longing, what zeal, what justice! In every way you showed yourselves to be pure in this matter. [12] So even though I wrote to you, it was not because of the one who did wrong, or because of the one who was wronged, but in order that your devotion to us might be made plain to you in the sight of God.

NOTES

JEPHTHAH'S VOW AND SACRIFICE

JEPHTHAH

Judges 10:6–12:7

RESCUE: 11:1–11:33
PEACE: NO REFERENCE

JUDGES 11

Jephthah Becomes Israel's Leader

¹ Jephthah the Gileadite was a valiant warrior, but he was the son of a prostitute, and Gilead was his father. ² Gilead's wife bore him sons, and when they grew up, they drove Jephthah out and said to him, "You will have no inheritance in our father's family, because you are the son of another woman." ³ So Jephthah fled from his brothers and lived in the land of Tob. Then some worthless men joined Jephthah and went on raids with him.

⁴ Some time later, the Ammonites fought against Israel. ⁵ When the Ammonites made war with Israel, the elders of Gilead went to get Jephthah from the land of Tob. ⁶ They said to him, "Come, be our commander, and let's fight the Ammonites."

⁷ Jephthah replied to the elders of Gilead, "Didn't you hate me and drive me out of my father's family? Why then have you come to me now when you're in trouble?"

⁸ They answered Jephthah, "That's true. But now we turn to you. Come with us, fight the Ammonites, and you will become leader of all the inhabitants of Gilead."

⁹ So Jephthah said to them, "If you are bringing me back to fight the Ammonites and the Lord gives them to me, I will be your leader."

¹⁰ The elders of Gilead said to Jephthah, "The Lord is our witness if we don't do as you say." ¹¹ So Jephthah went with the elders of Gilead. The people made him their leader and commander, and Jephthah repeated all his terms in the presence of the Lord at Mizpah.

Jephthah Rejects Ammonite Claims

12 Jephthah sent messengers to the king of the Ammonites, asking, "What do you have against me that you have come to fight me in my land?"

13 The king of the Ammonites said to Jephthah's messengers, "When Israel came from Egypt, they seized my land from the Arnon to the Jabbok and the Jordan. Now restore it peaceably."

14 Jephthah again sent messengers to the king of the Ammonites 15 to tell him, "This is what Jephthah says: Israel did not take away the land of Moab or the land of the Ammonites. 16 But when they came from Egypt, Israel traveled through the wilderness to the Red Sea and came to Kadesh. 17 Israel sent messengers to the king of Edom, saying, 'Please let us travel through your land,' but the king of Edom would not listen. They also sent messengers to the king of Moab, but he refused. So Israel stayed in Kadesh.

18 "Then they traveled through the wilderness and around the lands of Edom and Moab. They came to the east side of the land of Moab and camped on the other side of the Arnon but did not enter into the territory of Moab, for the Arnon was the boundary of Moab.

19 "Then Israel sent messengers to Sihon king of the Amorites, king of Heshbon. Israel said to him, 'Please let us travel through your land to our country,' 20 but Sihon would not trust Israel to pass through his territory. Instead, Sihon gathered all his troops, camped at Jahaz, and fought with Israel. 21 Then the LORD God of Israel handed over Sihon and all his troops to Israel, and they defeated them. So Israel took possession of the entire land of the Amorites who lived in that country. 22 They took possession of all the territory of the Amorites from the Arnon to the Jabbok and from the wilderness to the Jordan.

23 "The LORD God of Israel has now driven out the Amorites before his people Israel, and will you now force us out? 24 Isn't it true that you can have whatever your god Chemosh conquers for you, and we can have whatever the LORD our God conquers for us? 25 Now are you any better than Balak son of Zippor, king of Moab? Did he ever contend with Israel or fight against them? 26 While Israel lived three hundred years in Heshbon and Aroer and their surrounding villages, and in all the cities that are on the banks of the Arnon, why didn't you take them back at that time? 27 I have not sinned against you, but you are doing me wrong by fighting against me. Let the LORD who is the judge decide today between the Israelites and the Ammonites." 28 But the king of the Ammonites would not listen to Jephthah's message that he sent him.

Jephthah's Vow and Sacrifice

29 The Spirit of the LORD came on Jephthah, who traveled through Gilead and Manasseh, and then through Mizpah of Gilead. He crossed over to the Ammonites from Mizpah of Gilead. 30 Jephthah made this vow to the LORD: "If you in fact hand over the Ammonites to me, 31 whoever comes out the doors of my house to greet me when I return safely from the Ammonites will belong to the LORD, and I will offer that person as a burnt offering."

32 Jephthah crossed over to the Ammonites to fight against them, and the LORD handed them over to him. 33 He defeated twenty of their cities with a great slaughter from Aroer all the way to the entrance of Minnith and to Abel-keramim. So the Ammonites were subdued before the Israelites.

34 When Jephthah went to his home in Mizpah, there was his daughter, coming out to meet him with tambourines and dancing! She was his only child; he had no other son or daughter besides her. 35 When he saw her, he tore his clothes and said, "No! Not my daughter! You have devastated me! You have brought great misery on me. I have given my word to the LORD and cannot take it back."

36 Then she said to him, "My father, you have given your word to the LORD. Do to me as you have said, for the LORD brought vengeance on your enemies, the Ammonites." 37 She also said to her father, "Let me do this one thing: Let me

wander two months through the mountains with my friends and mourn my virginity."

[38] "Go," he said. And he sent her away two months. So she left with her friends and mourned her virginity as she wandered through the mountains. [39] At the end of two months, she returned to her father, and he kept the vow he had made about her. And she had never been intimate with a man. Now it became a custom in Israel [40] that four days each year the young women of Israel would commemorate the daughter of Jephthah the Gileadite.

♥ GOING DEEPER

PSALM 51
A Prayer for Restoration

For the choir director. A psalm of David, when the prophet Nathan came to him after he had gone to Bathsheba.

[1] Be gracious to me, God,
according to your faithful love;
according to your abundant compassion,
blot out my rebellion.
[2] Completely wash away my guilt
and cleanse me from my sin.
[3] For I am conscious of my rebellion,
and my sin is always before me.
[4] Against you—you alone—I have sinned
and done this evil in your sight.
So you are right when you pass sentence;
you are blameless when you judge.
[5] Indeed, I was guilty when I was born;
I was sinful when my mother conceived me.

[6] Surely you desire integrity in the inner self,
and you teach me wisdom deep within.
[7] Purify me with hyssop, and I will be clean;
wash me, and I will be whiter than snow.
[8] Let me hear joy and gladness;
let the bones you have crushed rejoice.

[9] Turn your face away from my sins
and blot out all my guilt.

[10] God, create a clean heart for me and renew a steadfast spirit within me.

[11] Do not banish me from your presence
or take your Holy Spirit from me.
[12] Restore the joy of your salvation to me,
and sustain me by giving me a willing spirit.
[13] Then I will teach the rebellious your ways,
and sinners will return to you.

[14] Save me from the guilt of bloodshed, God—
God of my salvation—
and my tongue will sing of your righteousness.
[15] Lord, open my lips,
and my mouth will declare your praise.
[16] You do not want a sacrifice, or I would give it;
you are not pleased with a burnt offering.
[17] The sacrifice pleasing to God is a broken spirit.
You will not despise a broken and humbled heart, God.

[18] In your good pleasure, cause Zion to prosper;
build the walls of Jerusalem.
[19] Then you will delight in righteous sacrifices,
whole burnt offerings;
then bulls will be offered on your altar.

MATTHEW 5:34–37

[34] "But I tell you, don't take an oath at all: either by heaven, because it is God's throne; [35] or by the earth, because it is his footstool; or by Jerusalem, because it is the city of the great King. [36] Do not swear by your head, because you cannot make a single hair white or black. [37] But let your 'yes' mean 'yes,' and your 'no' mean 'no.' Anything more than this is from the evil one."

THE CANAANITE RELIGION AND THE GOD OF ISRAEL

Before the people of Israel entered the promised land, the Lord warned them not to embrace the religion of the Canaanites.

When you enter the land the LORD your God is giving you, do not imitate the detestable customs of those nations. No one among you is to sacrifice his son or daughter in the fire, practice divination, tell fortunes, interpret omens, practice sorcery, cast spells, consult a medium or a spiritist, or inquire of the dead. Everyone who does these acts is detestable to the LORD, and the LORD your God is driving out the nations before you because of these detestable acts. You must be blameless before the LORD your God. Though these nations you are about to drive out listen to fortune-tellers and diviners, the LORD your God has not permitted you to do this.

DEUTERONOMY 18:9–14

The book of Judges begins with the somber admission that Israel embraced the Canaanite religion in spite of God's warning.

The Israelites did what was evil in the LORD's sight. They worshiped the Baals and abandoned the LORD, the God of their ancestors, who had brought them out of Egypt. They followed other gods from the surrounding peoples and bowed down to them. They angered the LORD, for they abandoned him and worshiped Baal and the Ashtoreths.

JUDGES 2:11–13

This rejection of God led to some of the most catastrophic and sad stories in Scripture. This chart contrasts some of the many differences between the Canaanite religion and the law of the God of Israel.

THE CANAANITE RELIGION	THE LAW OF GOD
Recognized several dozen gods	Recognized only one God, the Lord alone DT 5:7; 6:13–14
Had many idols and graven images	Forbade idols and graven images EX 20:4; LV 26:1; DT 5:8–10
Utilized many shrines and temples	Recognized only one tabernacle, the dwelling place of the Lord EX 25:9; 40:34–38; LV 19:30
Taught that different gods controlled different aspects of life and the world, like fertility, harvest, and war	Taught that the Lord created and maintains control over everything DT 4:19, 32–39
Embraced the practices of divination and sorcery	Forbade divination and sorcery LV 19:26; 20:6
Embraced the practice of child sacrifice	Forbade child sacrifice LV 18:21; DT 18:10
Embraced the practice of cult prostitution	Forbade cult prostitution LV 19:29; DT 23:17–18

13 / 28

GRACE DAY

Take this day to catch up on your reading, pray, and rest in the presence of the Lord.

Each Saturday we are turning from the tragedy of Judges to the hope of the gospel in Psalm 32, a psalm about joy and forgiveness.

PSALM 32:3–5

When I kept silent, my bones
  became brittle
from my groaning all day long.
For day and night your hand was
  heavy on me;
my strength was drained
as in the summer's heat.   *Selah*
Then I acknowledged my sin to you
and did not conceal my iniquity.
I said, "I will confess my transgressions to
  the LORD,"
and you forgave the guilt of my sin.
  Selah

Scripture is God-breathed and true. When we memorize it,
we carry His Word with us wherever we go.

This week we'll continue to memorize Judges 2:11–12a.
We'll memorize the rest of verse 11 and part of verse 12,
a reminder of how God's people continued to abandon
Him for other gods.

¹¹ The Israelites did what was evil in the Lᴏʀᴅ's sight. <u>They worshiped the Baals ¹² and abandoned the Lᴏʀᴅ,</u> the God of their ancestors, who had brought them out of Egypt.

See tips for memorizing Scripture on page 124.

I took my life in my own hands...

JUDGES 12:3

CONFLICT WITH EPHRAIM

JUDGES 12

¹ The men of Ephraim were called together and crossed the Jordan to Zaphon. They said to Jephthah, "Why have you crossed over to fight against the Ammonites but didn't call us to go with you? We will burn your house with you in it!"

² Then Jephthah said to them, "My people and I had a bitter conflict with the Ammonites. So I called for you, but you didn't deliver me from their power. ³ When I saw that you weren't going to deliver me, I took my life in my own hands and crossed over to the Ammonites, and the LORD handed them over to me. Why then have you come today to fight against me?"

⁴ Then Jephthah gathered all of the men of Gilead. They fought and defeated Ephraim, because Ephraim had said, "You Gileadites are Ephraimite fugitives in the territories of Ephraim and Manasseh." ⁵ The Gileadites captured the fords of the Jordan leading to Ephraim. Whenever a fugitive from Ephraim said, "Let me cross over," the Gileadites asked him, "Are you an Ephraimite?" If he answered, "No," ⁶ they told him, "Please say Shibboleth." If he said, "Sibboleth," because he could not pronounce it correctly, they seized him and executed him at the fords of the Jordan. At that time forty-two thousand from Ephraim died.

⁷ Jephthah judged Israel six years, and when he died, he was buried in one of the cities of Gilead.

Ibzan, Elon, and Abdon

[8] Ibzan, who was from Bethlehem, judged Israel after Jephthah [9] and had thirty sons. He gave his thirty daughters in marriage to men outside the tribe and brought back thirty wives for his sons from outside the tribe. Ibzan judged Israel seven years, [10] and when he died, he was buried in Bethlehem.

[11] Elon, who was from Zebulun, judged Israel after Ibzan. He judged Israel ten years, [12] and when he died, he was buried in Aijalon in the land of Zebulun.

[13] After Elon, Abdon son of Hillel, who was from Pirathon, judged Israel. [14] He had forty sons and thirty grandsons, who rode on seventy donkeys. Abdon judged Israel eight years, [15] and when he died, he was buried in Pirathon in the land of Ephraim, in the hill country of the Amalekites.

♥ GOING DEEPER

PROVERBS 24:1-22

[1] Don't envy the evil
or desire to be with them,
[2] for their hearts plan violence,
and their words stir up trouble.

[3] A house is built by wisdom,
and it is established by understanding;
[4] by knowledge the rooms are filled
with every precious and beautiful treasure.

[5] A wise warrior is better than a strong one,
and a man of knowledge than one of strength;
[6] for you should wage war with sound guidance—
victory comes with many counselors.

[7] Wisdom is inaccessible to a fool;
he does not open his mouth at the city gate.

[8] The one who plots evil
will be called a schemer.
[9] A foolish scheme is sin,
and a mocker is detestable to people.

[10] If you do nothing in a difficult time,
your strength is limited.
[11] Rescue those being taken off to death,
and save those stumbling toward slaughter.
[12] If you say, "But we didn't know about this,"
won't he who weighs hearts consider it?
Won't he who protects your life know?
Won't he repay a person according to his work?

[13] Eat honey, my son, for it is good,
and the honeycomb is sweet to your palate;
[14] realize that wisdom is the same for you.
If you find it, you will have a future,
and your hope will never fade.

[15] Don't set an ambush, you wicked one,
at the camp of the righteous man;
don't destroy his dwelling.
[16] Though a righteous person falls seven times,
he will get up,
but the wicked will stumble into ruin.

[17] Don't gloat when your enemy falls,
and don't let your heart rejoice when
    he stumbles,
[18] or the LORD will see, be displeased,
and turn his wrath away from him.

¹⁹ Don't be agitated by evildoers,
and don't envy the wicked.
²⁰ For the evil have no future;
the lamp of the wicked will be put out.

²¹ My son, fear the LORD, as well as the king,
and don't associate with rebels,
²² for destruction will come suddenly from them;
who knows what distress these two can bring?

ROMANS 12:9–21

⁹ Let love be without hypocrisy. Detest evil; cling to what is good. ¹⁰ Love one another deeply as brothers and sisters. Take the lead in honoring one another. ¹¹ Do not lack diligence in zeal; be fervent in the Spirit; serve the Lord. ¹² Rejoice in hope; be patient in affliction; be persistent in prayer. ¹³ Share with the saints in their needs; pursue hospitality. ¹⁴ Bless those who persecute you; bless and do not curse. ¹⁵ Rejoice with those who rejoice; weep with those who weep. ¹⁶ Live in harmony with one another. Do not be proud; instead, associate with the humble. Do not be wise in your own estimation. ¹⁷ Do not repay anyone evil for evil. Give careful thought to do what is honorable in everyone's eyes. ¹⁸ If possible, as far as it depends on you, live at peace with everyone. ¹⁹ Friends, do not avenge yourselves; instead, leave room for God's wrath, because it is written, Vengeance belongs to me; I will repay, says the Lord. ²⁰ But

If your enemy is hungry, feed him.
If he is thirsty, give him something to drink.
For in so doing
you will be heaping fiery coals on his head.

²¹ Do not be conquered by evil, but conquer evil with good.

THE BIRTH OF SAMSON

SAMSON
Judges 13–16

REBELLION: 13:1
OPPRESSION: 13:1
CRY FOR HELP:
13:2–23

JUDGES 13
Birth of Samson

¹ The Israelites again did what was evil in the LORD's sight, so the LORD handed them over to the Philistines forty years. ² There was a certain man from Zorah, from the family of Dan, whose name was Manoah; his wife was unable to conceive and had no children. ³ The angel of the LORD appeared to the woman and said to her, "Although you are unable to conceive and have no children, you will conceive and give birth to a son. ⁴ Now please be careful not to drink wine or beer, or to eat anything unclean; ⁵ for indeed, you will conceive and give birth to a son. You must never cut his hair, because the boy will be a Nazirite to God from birth, and he will begin to save Israel from the power of the Philistines."

⁶ Then the woman went and told her husband, "A man of God came to me. He looked like the awe-inspiring angel of God. I didn't ask him where he came from, and he didn't tell me his name. ⁷ He said to me, 'You will conceive and give birth to a son. Therefore, do not drink wine or beer, and do not eat anything unclean, because the boy will be a Nazirite to God from birth until the day of his death.'"

⁸ Manoah prayed to the LORD and said, "Please, Lord, let the man of God you sent come again to us and teach us what we should do for the boy who will be born."

⁹ God listened to Manoah, and the angel of God came again to the woman. She was sitting in the field, and her husband, Manoah, was not with her. ¹⁰ The woman ran quickly to her husband and told him, "The man who came to me the other day has just come back!"

¹¹ So Manoah got up and followed his wife. When he came to the man, he asked, "Are you the man who spoke to my wife?"

"I am," he said.

¹² Then Manoah asked, "When your words come true, what will be the boy's responsibilities and work?"

¹³ The angel of the LORD answered Manoah, "Your wife needs to do everything I told her. ¹⁴ She must not eat anything that comes from the grapevine or drink wine or beer. And she must not eat anything unclean. Your wife must do everything I have commanded her."

¹⁵ "Please stay here," Manoah told him, "and we will prepare a young goat for you."

¹⁶ The angel of the LORD said to him, "If I stay, I won't eat your food. But if you want to prepare a burnt offering, offer it to the LORD." (Manoah did not know he was the angel of the LORD.)

¹⁷ Then Manoah said to him, "What is your name, so that we may honor you when your words come true?"

¹⁸ "Why do you ask my name," the angel of the LORD asked him, "since it is beyond understanding?"

¹⁹ Manoah took a young goat and a grain offering and offered them on a rock to the LORD, who did something miraculous while Manoah and his wife were watching. ²⁰ When the flame went up from the altar to the sky, the angel of the LORD went up in its flame. When Manoah and his wife saw this, they fell facedown on the ground. ²¹ The angel of the LORD did not appear again to Manoah and his wife. Then Manoah realized that it was the angel of the LORD.

²² "We're certainly going to die," he said to his wife, "because we have seen God!"

²³ But his wife said to him, "If the LORD had intended to kill us, he wouldn't have accepted the burnt offering and the grain offering from us, and he would not have shown us all these things or spoken to us like this."

SAMSON

Judges 13:1–16:31

RESCUE: 13:24–16:31
PEACE: NO REFERENCE

²⁴ So the woman gave birth to a son and named him Samson. The boy grew, and the Lord blessed him. ²⁵ Then the Spirit of the Lord began to stir him in the Camp of Dan, between Zorah and Eshtaol.

⬥ GOING DEEPER

NUMBERS 6:1–12
The Nazirite Vow

¹ The Lord instructed Moses, ² "Speak to the Israelites and tell them: When a man or woman makes a special vow, a Nazirite vow, to consecrate himself to the Lord, ³ he is to abstain from wine and beer. He must not drink vinegar made from wine or from beer. He must not drink any grape juice or eat fresh grapes or raisins. ⁴ He is not to eat anything produced by the grapevine, from seeds to skin, during the period of his consecration.

⁵ "You must not cut his hair throughout the time of his vow of consecration. He may be holy until the time is completed during which he consecrates himself to the Lord; he is to let the hair of his head grow long. ⁶ He must not go near a dead body during the time he consecrates himself to the Lord. ⁷ He is not to defile himself for his father or mother, or his brother or sister, when they die, while the mark of consecration to his God is on his head.

⁸ He is holy to the Lord during the time of consecration.

⁹ "If someone suddenly dies near him, defiling his consecrated head, he must shave his head on the day of his purification; he is to shave it on the seventh day. ¹⁰ On the eighth day he is to bring two turtledoves or two young pigeons to the priest at the entrance to the tent of meeting. ¹¹ The priest is to offer one as a sin offering and the other as a burnt offering to make atonement on behalf of the Nazirite, since he incurred guilt because of the corpse. On that day he is to consecrate his head again. ¹² He is to rededicate his time of consecration to the Lord and to bring a year-old male lamb as a guilt offering. But do not count the initial period of consecration because it became defiled."

ROMANS 12:1

Therefore, brothers and sisters, in view of the mercies of God, I urge you to present your bodies as a living sacrifice, holy and pleasing to God; this is your true worship.

NOTES

SAMSON'S RIDDLE

JUDGES 14
Samson's Riddle

¹ Samson went down to Timnah and saw a young Philistine woman there. ² He went back and told his father and his mother, "I have seen a young Philistine woman in Timnah. Now get her for me as a wife."

³ But his father and mother said to him, "Can't you find a young woman among your relatives or among any of our people? Must you go to the uncircumcised Philistines for a wife?"

But Samson told his father, "Get her for me. She's the right one for me." ⁴ Now his father and mother did not know this was from the LORD, who wanted the Philistines to provide an opportunity for a confrontation. At that time, the Philistines were ruling Israel.

⁵ Samson went down to Timnah with his father and mother and came to the vineyards of Timnah. Suddenly a young lion came roaring at him, ⁶ the Spirit of the LORD came powerfully on him, and he tore the lion apart with his bare hands as he might have torn a young goat. But he did not tell his father or mother what he had done. ⁷ Then he went and spoke to the woman, because she seemed right to Samson.

⁸ After some time, when he returned to marry her, he left the road to see the lion's carcass, and there was a swarm of bees with honey in the carcass. ⁹ He scooped some honey into his hands and ate it as he went along. When he came to his father and mother, he gave some to them and they ate it. But

he did not tell them that he had scooped the honey from the lion's carcass.

¹⁰ His father went to visit the woman, and Samson prepared a feast there, as young men were accustomed to do. ¹¹ When the Philistines saw him, they brought thirty men to accompany him.

¹² "Let me tell you a riddle," Samson said to them. "If you can explain it to me during the seven days of the feast and figure it out, I will give you thirty linen garments and thirty changes of clothes. ¹³ But if you can't explain it to me, you must give me thirty linen garments and thirty changes of clothes."

"Tell us your riddle," they replied. "Let's hear it."

¹⁴ So he said to them:

Out of the eater came something to eat,
and out of the strong came something sweet.

After three days, they were unable to explain the riddle. ¹⁵ On the fourth day they said to Samson's wife, "Persuade your husband to explain the riddle to us, or we will burn you and your father's family to death. Did you invite us here to rob us?"

¹⁶ So Samson's wife came to him, weeping, and said, "You hate me and don't love me! You told my people the riddle, but haven't explained it to me."

"Look," he said, "I haven't even explained it to my father or mother, so why should I explain it to you?"

¹⁷ She wept the whole seven days of the feast, and at last, on the seventh day, he explained it to her, because she had nagged him so much. Then she explained it to her people.

¹⁸ On the seventh day, before sunset, the men of the city said to him:

What is sweeter than honey?
What is stronger than a lion?

So he said to them:

If you hadn't plowed with my young cow,
you wouldn't know my riddle now!

¹⁹ The Spirit of the LORD came powerfully on him, and he went down to Ashkelon and killed thirty of their men. He stripped them and gave their clothes to those who had explained the riddle. In a rage, Samson returned to his father's house, ²⁰ and his wife was given to one of the men who had accompanied him.

◆ GOING DEEPER

ISAIAH 11:1–5

¹ Then a shoot will grow from the stump of Jesse,
and a branch from his roots will bear fruit.
² The Spirit of the LORD will rest on him—
a Spirit of wisdom and understanding,
a Spirit of counsel and strength,
a Spirit of knowledge and of the fear of the LORD.
³ His delight will be in the fear of the LORD.
He will not judge
by what he sees with his eyes,
he will not execute justice
by what he hears with his ears,
⁴ but he will judge the poor righteously
and execute justice for the oppressed of the land.
He will strike the land
with a scepter from his mouth,

and he will kill the wicked
with a command from his lips.
⁵ Righteousness will be a belt around his hips;
faithfulness will be a belt around his waist.

MATTHEW 13:10–17
Why Jesus Used Parables

¹⁰ Then the disciples came up and asked him, "Why are you speaking to them in parables?"

¹¹ He answered, "Because the secrets of the kingdom of heaven have been given for you to know, but it has not been given to them. ¹² For whoever has, more will be given to him, and he will have more than enough; but whoever does not have, even what he has will be taken away from him. ¹³ That is why I speak to them in parables, because looking they do not see, and hearing they do not listen or understand. ¹⁴ Isaiah's prophecy is fulfilled in them, which says:

You will listen and listen,
but never understand;
you will look and look,
but never perceive.
¹⁵ For this people's heart has grown callous;
their ears are hard of hearing,
and they have shut their eyes;
otherwise they might see with their eyes,
and hear with their ears, and
understand with their hearts,
and turn back—
and I would heal them.

¹⁶ "Blessed are your eyes because they do see, and your ears because they do hear. ¹⁷ For truly I tell you, many prophets and righteous people longed to see the things you see but didn't see them, to hear the things you hear but didn't hear them."

SAMSON'S REVENGE

JUDGES 15
Samson's Revenge

¹ Later on, during the wheat harvest, Samson took a young goat as a gift and visited his wife. "I want to go to my wife in her room," he said. But her father would not let him enter.

² "I was sure you hated her," her father said, "so I gave her to one of the men who accompanied you. Isn't her younger sister more beautiful than she is? Why not take her instead?"

³ Samson said to them, "This time I will be blameless when I harm the Philistines." ⁴ So he went out and caught three hundred foxes. He took torches, turned the foxes tail-to-tail, and put a torch between each pair of tails. ⁵ Then he ignited the torches and released the foxes into the standing grain of the Philistines. He burned the piles of grain and the standing grain as well as the vineyards and olive groves.

⁶ Then the Philistines asked, "Who did this?"

They were told, "It was Samson, the Timnite's son-in-law, because he took Samson's wife and gave her to his companion." So the Philistines went to her and her father and burned them to death.

⁷ Then Samson told them, "Because you did this, I swear that I won't rest until I have taken vengeance on you." ⁸ He tore them limb from limb and then went down and stayed in the cave at the rock of Etam.

⁹ The Philistines went up, camped in Judah, and raided Lehi. ¹⁰ So the men of Judah said, "Why have you attacked us?"

They replied, "We have come to tie Samson up and pay him back for what he did to us."

¹¹ Then three thousand men of Judah went to the cave at the rock of Etam, and they asked Samson, "Don't you realize that the Philistines rule us? What have you done to us?"

"I have done to them what they did to me," he answered.

¹² They said to him, "We've come to tie you up and hand you over to the Philistines."

Then Samson told them, "Swear to me that you yourselves won't kill me."

¹³ "No," they said, "we won't kill you, but we will tie you up securely and hand you over to them." So they tied him up with two new ropes and led him away from the rock.

¹⁴ When he came to Lehi, the Philistines came to meet him shouting. The Spirit of the LORD came powerfully on him, and the ropes that were on his arms and wrists became like burnt flax and fell off. ¹⁵ He found a fresh jawbone of a donkey, reached out his hand, took it, and killed a thousand men with it. ¹⁶ Then Samson said:

With the jawbone of a donkey
I have piled them in heaps.
With the jawbone of a donkey
I have killed a thousand men.

¹⁷ When he finished speaking, he threw away the jawbone and named that place Jawbone Hill. ¹⁸ He became very thirsty and called out to the LORD, "You have accomplished this great victory through your servant. Must I now die of thirst and fall into the hands of the uncircumcised?" ¹⁹ So God split a hollow place in the ground at Lehi, and water came out of it. After Samson drank, his strength returned, and he revived. That is why he named it Hakkore Spring, which is still in Lehi today. ²⁰ And he judged Israel twenty years in the days of the Philistines.

❦ GOING DEEPER

PSALM 106:40–48

⁴⁰ Therefore the LORD's anger burned against his people,
and he abhorred his own inheritance.
⁴¹ He handed them over to the nations;
those who hated them ruled over them.
⁴² Their enemies oppressed them,
and they were subdued under their power.
⁴³ He rescued them many times,
but they continued to rebel deliberately
and were beaten down by their iniquity.

⁴⁴ When he heard their cry,
he took note of their distress,
⁴⁵ remembered his covenant with them,
and relented according to the abundance
of his faithful love.
⁴⁶ He caused them to be pitied
before all their captors.

⁴⁷ Save us, LORD our God,
and gather us from the nations,
so that we may give thanks to your holy name
and rejoice in your praise.

⁴⁸ Blessed be the LORD God of Israel,
from everlasting to everlasting.
Let all the people say, "Amen!"
Hallelujah!

HEBREWS 10:26–39
Warning Against Deliberate Sin
²⁶ For if we deliberately go on sinning after receiving the knowledge of the truth, there no longer remains a sacrifice

for sins, [27] but a terrifying expectation of judgment and the fury of a fire about to consume the adversaries. [28] Anyone who disregarded the law of Moses died without mercy, based on the testimony of two or three witnesses. [29] How much worse punishment do you think one will deserve who has trampled on the Son of God, who has regarded as profane the blood of the covenant by which he was sanctified, and who has insulted the Spirit of grace? [30] For we know the one who has said,

Vengeance belongs to me; I will repay,

and again,

The Lord will judge his people.

[31] It is a terrifying thing to fall into the hands of the living God.

[32] Remember the earlier days when, after you had been enlightened, you endured a hard struggle with sufferings. [33] Sometimes you were publicly exposed to taunts and afflictions, and at other times you were companions of those who were treated that way. [34] For you sympathized with the prisoners and accepted with joy the confiscation of your possessions, because you know that you yourselves have a better and enduring possession. [35] So don't throw away your confidence, which has a great reward. [36] For you need endurance, so that after you have done God's will, you may receive what was promised.

[37] For yet in a very little while,
the Coming One will come and not delay.
[38] But my righteous one will live by faith;
and if he draws back,
I have no pleasure in him.

[39] **But we are not those who draw back and are destroyed, but those who have faith and are saved.**

SAMSON'S DEFEAT AND DEATH

JUDGES 16
Samson and Delilah

[1] Samson went to Gaza, where he saw a prostitute and went to bed with her. [2] When the Gazites heard that Samson was there, they surrounded the place and waited in ambush for him all that night at the city gate. They kept quiet all night, saying, "Let's wait until dawn; then we will kill him." [3] But Samson stayed in bed only until midnight. Then he got up, took hold of the doors of the city gate along with the two gateposts, and pulled them out, bar and all. He put them on his shoulders and took them to the top of the mountain overlooking Hebron.

[4] Some time later, he fell in love with a woman named Delilah, who lived in the Sorek Valley. [5] The Philistine leaders went to her and said, "Persuade him to tell you where his great strength comes from, so we can overpower him, tie him up, and make him helpless. Each of us will then give you 1,100 pieces of silver."

[6] So Delilah said to Samson, "Please tell me, where does your great strength come from? How could someone tie you up and make you helpless?"

7 Samson told her, "If they tie me up with seven fresh bowstrings that have not been dried, I will become weak and be like any other man."

8 The Philistine leaders brought her seven fresh bowstrings that had not been dried, and she tied him up with them. 9 While the men in ambush were waiting in her room, she called out to him, "Samson, the Philistines are here!" But he snapped the bowstrings as a strand of yarn snaps when it touches fire. The secret of his strength remained unknown.

10 Then Delilah said to Samson, "You have mocked me and told me lies! Won't you please tell me how you can be tied up?"

11 He told her, "If they tie me up with new ropes that have never been used, I will become weak and be like any other man."

12 Delilah took new ropes, tied him up with them, and shouted, "Samson, the Philistines are here!" But while the men in ambush were waiting in her room, he snapped the ropes off his arms like a thread.

13 Then Delilah said to Samson, "You have mocked me all along and told me lies! Tell me how you can be tied up."

He told her, "If you weave the seven braids on my head into the fabric on a loom—"

14 She fastened the braids with a pin and called to him, "Samson, the Philistines are here!" He awoke from his sleep and pulled out the pin, with the loom and the web.

15 "How can you say, 'I love you,'" she told him, "when your heart is not with me? This is the third time you have mocked me and not told me what makes your strength so great!"

16 Because she nagged him day after day and pleaded with him until she wore him out, 17 he told her the whole truth and said to her, "My hair has never been cut, because I am a Nazirite to God from birth. If I am shaved, my strength will leave me, and I will become weak and be like any other man."

18 When Delilah realized that he had told her the whole truth, she sent this message to the Philistine leaders: "Come one more time, for he has told me the whole truth." The Philistine leaders came to her and brought the silver with them.

19 Then she let him fall asleep on her lap and called a man to shave off the seven braids on his head. In this way, she made him helpless, and his strength left him. 20 Then she cried, "Samson, the Philistines are here!" When he awoke from his sleep, he said, "I will escape as I did before and shake myself free." But he did not know that the Lord had left him.

Samson's Defeat and Death

21 The Philistines seized him and gouged out his eyes. They brought him down to Gaza and bound him with bronze shackles, and he was forced to grind grain in the prison. 22 But his hair began to grow back after it had been shaved.

23 Now the Philistine leaders gathered together to offer a great sacrifice to their god Dagon. They rejoiced and said:

Our god has handed over
our enemy Samson to us.

24 When the people saw him, they praised their god and said:

Our god has handed over to us
our enemy who destroyed our land
and who multiplied our dead.

25 When they were in good spirits, they said, "Bring Samson here to entertain us." So they brought Samson from prison, and he entertained them. They had him stand between the pillars.

26 Samson said to the young man who was leading him by the hand, "Lead me where I can feel the pillars supporting the temple, so I can lean against them." 27 The temple was full of men and women; all the leaders of the Philistines were there, and about three thousand men and women were on the roof watching Samson entertain them. 28 He called out to the Lord, "Lord God, please remember me. Strengthen me, God, just once more. With one act of vengeance, let me

pay back the Philistines for my two eyes." ²⁹ Samson took hold of the two middle pillars supporting the temple and leaned against them, one on his right hand and the other on his left. ³⁰ Samson said, "Let me die with the Philistines." He pushed with all his might, and the temple fell on the leaders and all the people in it. And those he killed at his death were more than those he had killed in his life.

³¹ Then his brothers and his father's whole family came down, carried him back, and buried him between Zorah and Eshtaol in the tomb of his father Manoah. So he judged Israel twenty years.

◆ GOING DEEPER

JEREMIAH 15:15–16
Jeremiah's Prayer for Vengeance
¹⁵ You know, Lord;
remember me and take note of me.
Avenge me against my persecutors.
In your patience, don't take me away.
Know that I suffer disgrace for your honor.

¹⁶ Your words were found, and I ate them. Your words became a delight to me and the joy of my heart, for I bear your name,

Lord God of Armies.

HEBREWS 11:32–38
³² And what more can I say? Time is too short for me to tell about Gideon, Barak, Samson, Jephthah, David, Samuel, and the prophets, ³³ who by faith conquered kingdoms, administered justice, obtained promises, shut the mouths of lions, ³⁴ quenched the raging of fire, escaped the edge of the sword, gained strength in weakness, became mighty in battle, and put foreign armies to flight. ³⁵ Women received their dead, raised to life again. Other people were tortured, not accepting release, so that they might gain a better resurrection. ³⁶ Others experienced mockings and scourgings, as well as bonds and imprisonment. ³⁷ They were stoned, they were sawed in two, they died by the sword, they wandered about in sheepskins, in goatskins, destitute, afflicted, and mistreated. ³⁸ The world was not worthy of them. They wandered in deserts and on mountains, hiding in caves and holes in the ground.

NOTES

THE JUDGES OF ISRAEL

Othniel — 40 years

Ehud — 80 years

Shamgar — Unspecified

Deborah — 40 years

Gideon — 40 years

Tola — 23 years

Jair — 22 years

Jephthah — 6

Ibzan — 7

Elon — 10

Abdon — 8

Samson — 20 years

Samuel — Around 80 years

Between the times of the patriarchs and the kings, the people of Israel experienced a season of transition before they developed into a nation. This was the time of the judges, when "there was no king in Israel; everyone did whatever seemed right to him" (Jdg 21:25). During this time, Israel suffered at the hands of invading armies, often because of their own rebellion. So "the LORD raised up judges, who saved them from the power of their marauders" (Jdg 2:16). Here is an overview of their leadership.

Othniel

Ended eight years of Canaanite oppression by defeating King Cushan-rishathaim.

40 YEARS // JDG 1:12–13; 3:7–11

Ehud

Ended eighteen years of oppression by defeating King Eglon of Moab and his army.

80 YEARS // JDG 3:12–30

Shamgar

Ended a season of Philistine oppression by killing six hundred Philistines with a cattle prod.

UNSPECIFIED YEARS // JDG 3:31

Deborah

Ended twenty years of oppression by convincing Barak to lead an army against the Canaanites.

40 YEARS // JDG 4–5

Gideon

Ended seven years of Midianite oppression by leading a band of three hundred men against 135,000 Midianites.

40 YEARS // JDG 6–8

Tola

Unspecified

23 YEARS // JDG 10:1–2

Jair

Unspecified

22 YEARS // JDG 10:3–5

Jephthah

Defeated the Ammonites after making a rash promise to the Lord.

6 YEARS // JDG 11:1–12:7

Ibzan

Unspecified

7 YEARS // JDG 12:8–10

Elon

Unspecified

10 YEARS // JDG 12:11–12

Abdon

Unspecified

8 YEARS // JDG 12:13–15

Samson

Ended forty years of Philistine oppression; killed a thousand Philistines with the jawbone of a donkey; lost his strength at the hands of Delilah; destroyed a Philistine temple.

20 YEARS // JDG 13–16

Samuel

The last judge and the first prophet; anointed Israel's first two kings, Saul and David.

AROUND 80 YEARS // 1SM 1:1–25:1

20 / 28

GRACE DAY

Take this day to catch up on your reading, pray, and rest in the presence of the Lord.

Each Saturday we are turning from the tragedy of Judges to the hope of the gospel in Psalm 32, a psalm about joy and forgiveness.

PSALM 32:6–7

Therefore let everyone who is
    faithful pray to you immediately.
When great floodwaters come,
they will not reach him.
You are my hiding place;
you protect me from trouble.
You surround me with joyful shouts
    of deliverance.   *Selah*

Scripture is God-breathed and true. When we memorize it,
we carry His Word with us wherever we go.

We'll commit the final portion of Judges 2:11–12a to memory
this week. It points us to who God is and how He has
rescued His people in the past.

¹¹ The Israelites did what was evil in the LORD's sight. They worshiped the Baals ¹² and abandoned the LORD, <u>the God of their ancestors, who had brought them out of Egypt.</u>

See tips for memorizing Scripture on page 124.

Everyone DID whatever Seemed right TO HIM.

JUDGES 17:6

MICAH'S PRIEST

JUDGES 17
Micah's Priest

[1] There was a man from the hill country of Ephraim named Micah. [2] He said to his mother, "The 1,100 pieces of silver taken from you, and that I heard you place a curse on—here's the silver. I took it."

Then his mother said, "My son, may you be blessed by the LORD!"

[3] He returned the 1,100 pieces of silver to his mother, and his mother said, "I personally consecrate the silver to the LORD for my son's benefit to make a carved image and a silver idol. I will give it back to you." [4] So he returned the silver to his mother, and she took five pounds of silver and gave it to a silversmith. He made it into a carved image and a silver idol, and it was in Micah's house.

[5] This man Micah had a shrine, and he made an ephod and household idols, and installed one of his sons to be his priest. [6] In those days there was no king in Israel; everyone did whatever seemed right to him.

[7] There was a young man, a Levite from Bethlehem in Judah, who was staying within the clan of Judah. [8] The man left the town of Bethlehem in Judah to stay wherever he could find a place. On his way he came to Micah's home in the hill country of Ephraim.

[9] "Where do you come from?" Micah asked him.

He answered him, "I am a Levite from Bethlehem in Judah, and I'm going to stay wherever I can find a place."

¹⁰ Micah replied, "Stay with me and be my father and priest, and I will give you four ounces of silver a year, along with your clothing and provisions." So the Levite went in ¹¹ and agreed to stay with the man, and the young man became like one of his sons. ¹² Micah consecrated the Levite, and the young man became his priest and lived in Micah's house. ¹³ Then Micah said, "Now I know that the Lord will be good to me, because a Levite has become my priest."

◗ GOING DEEPER

EXODUS 20:4–6

⁴ "Do not make an idol for yourself, whether in the shape of anything in the heavens above or on the earth below or in the waters under the earth. ⁵ Do not bow in worship to them, and do not serve them; for I, the Lord your God, am a jealous God, bringing the consequences of the fathers' iniquity on the children to the third and fourth generations of those who hate me, ⁶ but showing faithful love to a thousand generations of those who love me and keep my commands."

ACTS 17:24–31

²⁴ The God who made the world and everything in it—he is Lord of heaven and earth—does not live in shrines made by hands. ²⁵ Neither is he served by human hands, as though he needed anything, since he himself gives everyone life and breath and all things. ²⁶ From one man he has made every nationality to live over the whole earth and has determined their appointed times and the boundaries of where they live.

²⁷ He did this so that they might seek God, and perhaps they might reach out and find him, though he is not far from each one of us. ²⁸ For in him we live and move and have our being,

as even some of your own poets have said, "For we are also his offspring." ²⁹ Since, then, we are God's offspring, we shouldn't think that the divine nature is like gold or silver or stone, an image fashioned by human art and imagination.

³⁰ Therefore, having overlooked the times of ignorance, God now commands all people everywhere to repent, ³¹ because he has set a day when he is going to judge the world in righteousness by the man he has appointed. He has provided proof of this to everyone by raising him from the dead.

NOTES

DAN'S INVASION AND IDOLATRY

JUDGES 18
Dan's Invasion and Idolatry

¹ In those days, there was no king in Israel, and the Danite tribe was looking for territory to occupy. Up to that time no territory had been captured by them among the tribes of Israel. ² So the Danites sent out five brave men from all their clans, from Zorah and Eshtaol, to scout out the land and explore it. They told them, "Go and explore the land."

They came to the hill country of Ephraim as far as the home of Micah and spent the night there. ³ While they were near Micah's home, they recognized the accent of the young Levite. So they went over to him and asked, "Who brought you here? What are you doing in this place? What is keeping you here?"

⁴ He told them, "This is what Micah has done for me: He has hired me, and I became his priest."

⁵ Then they said to him, "Please inquire of God for us to determine if we will have a successful journey."

⁶ The priest told them, "Go in peace. The LORD is watching over the journey you are going on."

⁷ The five men left and came to Laish. They saw that the people who were there were living securely, in the same way as the Sidonians, quiet and unsuspecting. There was nothing lacking in the land and no oppressive ruler. They were far from the Sidonians, having no alliance with anyone.

⁸ When the men went back to their relatives at Zorah and Eshtaol, their relatives asked them, "What did you find out?"

9 They answered, "Come on, let's attack them, for we have seen the land, and it is very good. Why wait? Don't hesitate to go and invade and take possession of the land! 10 When you get there, you will come to an unsuspecting people and a spacious land, for God has handed it over to you. It is a place where nothing on earth is lacking." 11 Six hundred Danites departed from Zorah and Eshtaol armed with weapons of war. 12 They went up and camped at Kiriath-jearim in Judah. This is why the place is still called the Camp of Dan today; it is west of Kiriath-jearim. 13 From there they traveled to the hill country of Ephraim and arrived at Micah's house.

14 The five men who had gone to scout out the land of Laish told their brothers, "Did you know that there are an ephod, household gods, and a carved image and a silver idol in these houses? Now think about what you should do." 15 So they detoured there and went to the house of the young Levite at the home of Micah and greeted him. 16 The six hundred Danite men were standing by the entrance of the city gate, armed with their weapons of war. 17 Then the five men who had gone to scout out the land went in and took the carved image, the ephod, the household idols, and the silver idol, while the priest was standing by the entrance of the city gate with the six hundred men armed with weapons of war.

18 When they entered Micah's house and took the carved image, the ephod, the household idols, and the silver idol, the priest said to them, "What are you doing?"

19 They told him, "Be quiet. Keep your mouth shut. Come with us and be a father and a priest to us. Is it better for you to be a priest for the house of one person or for you to be a priest for a tribe and family in Israel?" 20 So the priest was pleased and took the ephod, household idols, and carved image, and went with the people. 21 They prepared to leave, putting their dependents, livestock, and possessions in front of them.

22 After they were some distance from Micah's house, the men who were in the houses near it were mustered and caught up with the Danites. 23 They called to the Danites, who turned to face them, and said to Micah, "What's the matter with you that you mustered the men?"

24 He said, "You took the gods I had made and the priest, and went away. What do I have left? How can you say to me, 'What's the matter with you?'"

25 The Danites said to him, "Don't raise your voice against us, or angry men will attack you, and you and your family will lose your lives." 26 The Danites went on their way, and Micah turned to go back home, because he saw that they were stronger than he was.

27 After they had taken the gods Micah had made and the priest that belonged to him, they went to Laish, to a quiet and unsuspecting people. They killed them with their swords and burned the city. 28 There was no one to rescue them because it was far from Sidon and they had no alliance with anyone. It was in a valley that belonged to Beth-rehob. They rebuilt the city and lived in it. 29 They named the city Dan, after the name of their ancestor Dan, who was born to Israel. The city was formerly named Laish.

30 The Danites set up the carved image for themselves. Jonathan son of Gershom, son of Moses, and his sons were priests for the Danite tribe until the time of the exile from the land. 31 So they set up for themselves Micah's carved image that he had made, and it was there as long as the house of God was in Shiloh.

🛡 GOING DEEPER

PSALM 78:56–66

56 But they rebelliously tested the Most High God,
for they did not keep his decrees.
57 They treacherously turned away like their ancestors;
they became warped like a faulty bow.
58 They enraged him with their high places
and provoked his jealousy with their carved images.
59 God heard and became furious;
he completely rejected Israel.
60 He abandoned the tabernacle at Shiloh,
the tent where he resided among mankind.
61 He gave up his strength to captivity
and his splendor to the hand of a foe.

⁶² He surrendered his people to the sword
because he was enraged with his heritage.
⁶³ Fire consumed his chosen young men,
and his young women had no wedding songs.
⁶⁴ His priests fell by the sword,
and the widows could not lament.

⁶⁵ The Lord awoke as if from sleep,
like a warrior from the effects of wine.
⁶⁶ He beat back his foes;
he gave them lasting disgrace.

1 PETER 1:17–23

¹⁷ If you appeal to the Father who judges impartially according to each one's work, you are to conduct yourselves in reverence during your time living as strangers.

¹⁸ **For you know that you were redeemed from your empty way of life inherited from your ancestors, not with perishable things like silver or gold, ¹⁹ but with the precious blood of Christ,**

like that of an unblemished and spotless lamb. ²⁰ He was foreknown before the foundation of the world but was revealed in these last times for you. ²¹ Through him you believe in God, who raised him from the dead and gave him glory, so that your faith and hope are in God.

²² Since you have purified yourselves by your obedience to the truth, so that you show sincere brotherly love for each other, from a pure heart love one another constantly, ²³ because you have been born again—not of perishable seed but of imperishable—through the living and enduring word of God.

WHAT IS A

Tragedy?

1. an event causing great suffering, destruction, and distress, such as a serious accident, crime, or natural catastrophe

2. a story, fiction or nonfiction, that deals with tragic events and has an unhappy ending, especially one involving the downfall of the main character[1]

The book of Judges is an account of true historical tragedy written in the form of literary tragedy. The series of events contained in the book tell of Israel's long spiral into depravity. Recognizing Judges as a tragedy—a narrative that ends with downfall—helps us make better sense of what we're reading.

Reading the genre of tragedy can be difficult because of the way it makes us face the reality of brokenness, suffering, and injustice in our world and our stories. When things are not as they should be, we ache for a reckoning or redemption. Here are some helpful things to remember as you reflect on this type of literature in Scripture.

[1] *Oxford English Dictionary.* "tragedy, n."

BIBLICAL NARRATIVE IS OFTEN DESCRIPTIVE RATHER THAN PRESCRIPTIVE.

The stories of God's people are not always positive or meant to be followed. Additionally, women and men in the Bible are complex and rarely fall into neat categories of "good" and "bad."

———

JESUS IS THE ONLY HOPE FOR EVERY STORY.

Because of Jesus's death, resurrection, and ascension, believers can trust God to redeem all that sin has broken, and that He will ultimately make all things new (Rv 21:3–5). As we are made uncomfortable by tragedy, we have the hope of the gospel to meet us there and give us peace (Jn 16:33).

———

WE CAN PARTICIPATE IN GOD'S PLAN TO RESTORE AND REDEEM.

Reading tragedy can be overwhelming and bring up feelings of helplessness as the genre addresses large amounts of suffering. As coheirs and coworkers with Christ, we can reflect the person and work of Jesus to a broken world and participate in His restoration as we are obedient to God's ways (Rm 8:12–27; 2Co 5:18–19).

OUTRAGE
IN BENJAMIN

JUDGES 19
Outrage in Benjamin

[1] In those days, when there was no king in Israel, a Levite staying in a remote part of the hill country of Ephraim acquired a woman from Bethlehem in Judah as his concubine. [2] But she was unfaithful to him and left him for her father's house in Bethlehem in Judah. She was there for four months. [3] Then her husband got up and followed her to speak kindly to her and bring her back. He had his servant with him and a pair of donkeys. So she brought him to her father's house, and when the girl's father saw him, he gladly welcomed him. [4] His father-in-law, the girl's father, detained him, and he stayed with him for three days. They ate, drank, and spent the nights there.

[5] On the fourth day, they got up early in the morning and prepared to go, but the girl's father said to his son-in-law, "Have something to eat to keep up your strength and then you can go." [6] So they sat down and the two of them ate and drank together. Then the girl's father said to the man, "Please agree to stay overnight and enjoy yourself." [7] The man got up to go, but his father-in-law persuaded him, so he stayed and spent the night there again. [8] He got up early in the morning of the fifth day to leave, but the girl's father said to him, "Please keep up your strength." So they waited until late afternoon and the two of them ate. [9] The man got up to go with his concubine and his servant, when his father-in-law, the girl's father, said to him, "Look, night is coming. Please spend the night. See, the day is almost over. Spend the night here, enjoy yourself, then you can get up early tomorrow for your journey and go home."

[10] But the man was unwilling to spend the night. He got up, departed, and arrived opposite Jebus (that is, Jerusalem). The man had his two saddled donkeys and his concubine with him. [11] When they were near Jebus and the day was almost gone, the

servant said to his master, "Please, why not let us stop at this Jebusite city and spend the night here?"

¹² But his master replied to him, "We will not stop at a foreign city where there are no Israelites. Let's move on to Gibeah." ¹³ "Come on," he said, "let's try to reach one of these places and spend the night in Gibeah or Ramah." ¹⁴ So they continued on their journey, and the sun set as they neared Gibeah in Benjamin. ¹⁵ They stopped to go in and spend the night in Gibeah. The Levite went in and sat down in the city square, but no one took them into their home to spend the night.

¹⁶ In the evening, an old man came in from his work in the field. He was from the hill country of Ephraim, but he was residing in Gibeah where the people were Benjaminites. ¹⁷ When he looked up and saw the traveler in the city square, the old man asked, "Where are you going, and where do you come from?"

¹⁸ He answered him, "We're traveling from Bethlehem in Judah to the remote hill country of Ephraim, where I am from. I went to Bethlehem in Judah, and now I'm going to the house of the LORD. No one has taken me into his home, ¹⁹ although there's straw and feed for the donkeys, and I have bread and wine for me, my concubine, and the servant with us. There is nothing we lack."

²⁰ "Welcome!" said the old man. "I'll take care of everything you need. Only don't spend the night in the square." ²¹ So he brought him to his house and fed the donkeys. Then they washed their feet and ate and drank. ²² While they were enjoying themselves, all of a sudden, wicked men of the city surrounded the house and beat on the door. They said to the old man who was the owner of the house, "Bring out the man who came to your house so we can have sex with him!"

²³ The owner of the house went out and said to them, "Please don't do this evil, my brothers. After all, this man has come into my house. Don't commit this horrible outrage. ²⁴ Here, let me bring out my virgin daughter and the man's concubine now. Abuse them and do whatever you want to them. But don't commit this outrageous thing against this man."

²⁵ But the men would not listen to him, so the man seized his concubine and took her outside to them. They raped her and abused her all night until morning. At daybreak they let her go. ²⁶ Early that morning, the woman made her way back, and as it was getting light, she collapsed at the doorway of the man's house where her master was.

²⁷ When her master got up in the morning, opened the doors of the house, and went out to leave on his journey, there was the woman, his concubine, collapsed near the doorway of the house with her hands on the threshold. ²⁸ "Get up," he told her. "Let's go." But there was no response. So the man put her on his donkey and set out for home.

²⁹ When he entered his house, he picked up a knife, took hold of his concubine, cut her into twelve pieces, limb by limb, and then sent her throughout the territory of Israel. ³⁰ Everyone who saw it said, "Nothing like this has ever happened or has been seen since the day the Israelites came out of the land of Egypt until now. Think it over, discuss it, and speak up!"

⬛ GOING DEEPER

JEREMIAH 8:18–22
Lament over Judah

¹⁸ My joy has flown away;
grief has settled on me.
My heart is sick.
¹⁹ Listen—the cry of my dear people
from a faraway land,
"Is the LORD no longer in Zion,
her King not within her?"
Why have they angered me
with their carved images,
with their worthless foreign idols?
²⁰ Harvest has passed, summer has ended,
but we have not been saved.
²¹ I am broken by the brokenness
of my dear people.
I mourn; horror has taken hold of me.
²² Is there no balm in Gilead?
Is there no physician there?

So why has the healing of my dear people
not come about?

JEREMIAH 9:1–3

[1] If my head were a flowing spring,
my eyes a fountain of tears,
I would weep day and night
over the slain of my dear people.
[2] If only I had a traveler's lodging place
in the wilderness,
I would abandon my people
and depart from them,
for they are all adulterers,
a solemn assembly of treacherous people.

[3] They bent their tongues like their bows;
lies and not faithfulness prevail in the land,
for they proceed from one evil to another,
and they do not take me into account.
This is the LORD's declaration.

2 CORINTHIANS 6:14–18
Separation to God

[14] Do not be yoked together with those who do not believe.
For what partnership is there between righteousness and
lawlessness? Or what fellowship does light have with darkness?
[15] What agreement does Christ have with Belial? Or what does
a believer have in common with an unbeliever? [16] And what
agreement does the temple of God have with idols? For we are
the temple of the living God, as God said:

I will dwell
and walk among them,
and I will be their God,
and they will be my people.
[17] Therefore, come out from among them
and be separate, says the Lord;
do not touch any unclean thing,
and I will welcome you.
[18] And I will be a Father to you,
and you will be sons and daughters to me,
says the Lord Almighty.

WAR AGAINST BENJAMIN

JUDGES 20
War Against Benjamin

¹ All the Israelites from Dan to Beer-sheba and from the land of Gilead came out, and the community assembled as one body before the LORD at Mizpah. ² The leaders of all the people and of all the tribes of Israel presented themselves in the assembly of God's people: four hundred thousand armed foot soldiers. ³ The Benjaminites heard that the Israelites had gone up to Mizpah.

The Israelites asked, "Tell us, how did this evil act happen?"

⁴ The Levite, the husband of the murdered woman, answered, "I went to Gibeah in Benjamin with my concubine to spend the night. ⁵ Citizens of Gibeah came to attack me and surrounded the house at night. They intended to kill me, but they raped my concubine, and she died. ⁶ Then I took my concubine and cut her in pieces, and sent her throughout Israel's territory, because they have committed a wicked outrage in Israel. ⁷ Look, all of you are Israelites. Give your judgment and verdict here and now."

⁸ Then all the people stood united and said, "None of us will go to his tent or return to his house. ⁹ Now this is what we will do to Gibeah: we will attack it. By lot ¹⁰ we will take ten men out of every hundred from all the tribes of Israel, and one hundred out of every thousand, and one thousand out of every ten thousand to get provisions for the troops when they go to Gibeah in Benjamin to punish them for all the outrage they committed in Israel."

¹¹ So all the men of Israel gathered united against the city. ¹² Then the tribes of Israel sent men throughout the tribe of Benjamin, saying, "What is this evil act that has happened among you? ¹³ Hand over the wicked men in Gibeah so we can put them to death and purge evil from Israel." But the Benjaminites would not listen to their fellow Israelites. ¹⁴ Instead, the Benjaminites gathered together from their cities to Gibeah to go out and fight against the Israelites. ¹⁵ On that day the Benjaminites mobilized twenty-six thousand armed men from their cities, besides seven hundred fit young men rallied by the inhabitants of Gibeah. ¹⁶ There were seven hundred fit young men who were left-handed among all these troops; all could sling a stone at a hair and not miss.

¹⁷ The Israelites, apart from Benjamin, mobilized four hundred thousand armed men, every one an experienced warrior. ¹⁸ They set out, went to Bethel, and inquired of God. The Israelites asked, "Who is to go first to fight for us against the Benjaminites?"

And the LORD answered, "Judah will be first."

¹⁹ In the morning, the Israelites set out and camped near Gibeah. ²⁰ The men of Israel went out to fight against Benjamin and took their battle positions against Gibeah. ²¹ The Benjaminites came out of Gibeah and slaughtered twenty-two thousand men of Israel on the field that day. ²² But the Israelite troops rallied and again took their battle positions in the same place where they positioned themselves on the first day. ²³ They went up, wept before the LORD until evening, and inquired of him, "Should we again attack our brothers the Benjaminites?"

And the LORD answered, "Fight against them."

²⁴ On the second day the Israelites advanced against the Benjaminites. ²⁵ That same day the Benjaminites came out from Gibeah to meet them and slaughtered an additional eighteen thousand Israelites on the field; all were armed.

²⁶ The whole Israelite army went to Bethel where they wept and sat before the LORD. They fasted that day until evening and offered burnt offerings and fellowship offerings to the LORD. ²⁷ Then the Israelites inquired of the LORD. In those days, the ark of the covenant of God was there, ²⁸ and Phinehas son of Eleazar, son of Aaron, was serving before it. The Israelites asked, "Should we again fight against our brothers the Benjaminites or should we stop?"

The LORD answered, "Fight, because I will hand them over to you tomorrow." ²⁹ So Israel set up an ambush around Gibeah. ³⁰ On the third day the Israelites fought against the Benjaminites and took their battle positions against Gibeah as before. ³¹ Then the Benjaminites came out against the troops and were drawn away from the city. They began to attack the troops as before, killing about thirty men of Israel on the highways, one of which goes up to Bethel and the other to Gibeah through the open country. ³² The Benjaminites said, "We are defeating them as before."

But the Israelites said, "Let's flee and draw them away from the city to the highways." ³³ So all the men of Israel got up from their places and took their battle positions at Baal-tamar, while the Israelites in ambush charged out of their places west of Geba. ³⁴ Then ten thousand fit young men from all Israel made a frontal assault against Gibeah, and the battle was fierce, but the Benjaminites did not know that disaster was about to strike them. ³⁵ The LORD defeated Benjamin in the presence of Israel, and on that day the Israelites slaughtered 25,100 men of Benjamin; all were armed. ³⁶ Then the Benjaminites realized they had been defeated.

The men of Israel had retreated before Benjamin, because they were confident in the ambush they had set against Gibeah. ³⁷ The men in ambush had rushed quickly against Gibeah; they advanced and put the whole city to the sword. ³⁸ The men of Israel had a prearranged signal with the men in ambush: when they sent up a great cloud of smoke from the city, [39] the men of Israel would return to the battle. When Benjamin had begun to strike them down, killing about thirty men of Israel, they said, "They're defeated before us, just as they were in the first battle." [40] But when the column of smoke began to go up from the city, Benjamin looked behind them, and the whole city was going up in smoke. [41] Then the men of Israel returned, and the men of Benjamin were terrified when they realized that disaster had struck them. [42] They retreated before the men of Israel toward the wilderness, but the battle overtook them, and those who came out of the cities slaughtered those between them. [43] They surrounded the Benjaminites, pursued them, and easily overtook them near Gibeah toward the east. [44] There were eighteen thousand men who died from Benjamin; all were warriors. [45] Then Benjamin turned and fled toward the wilderness to Rimmon Rock, and Israel killed five thousand men on the highways. They overtook them at Gidom and struck two thousand more dead.

[46] All the Benjaminites who died that day were twenty-five thousand armed men; all were warriors. [47] But six hundred men escaped into the wilderness to Rimmon Rock and stayed there four months. [48] The men of Israel turned back against the other Benjaminites and killed them with their swords—the entire city, the animals, and everything that remained. They also burned all the cities that remained.

◗ **GOING DEEPER**

LAMENTATIONS 1:18, 22
צ Tsade
[18] The LORD is just,
for I have rebelled against his command.
Listen, all you people;
look at my pain.
My young women and young men
have gone into captivity.

. . .

ת Taw
[22] Let all their wickedness come before you,
and deal with them
as you have dealt with me
because of all my transgressions.
For my groans are many,
and I am sick at heart.

ROMANS 2:2–10
[2] Now we know that God's judgment on those who do such things is based on the truth. [3] Do you think—anyone of you who judges those who do such things yet do the same—that you will escape God's judgment? [4] Or do you despise the riches of his kindness, restraint, and patience, not recognizing that God's kindness is intended to lead you to repentance? [5] Because of your hardened and unrepentant heart you are storing up wrath for yourself in the day of wrath, when God's righteous judgment is revealed.

[6] He will repay each one according to his works:

[7] eternal life to those who by persistence in doing wgood seek glory, honor, and immortality; [8] but wrath and anger to those who are self-seeking and disobey the truth while obeying unrighteousness. [9] There will be affliction and distress for every human being who does evil, first to the Jew, and also to the Greek; [10] but glory, honor, and peace for everyone who does what is good, first to the Jew, and also to the Greek.

NOTES

BRIDES FOR BENJAMIN

JUDGES 21
Brides for Benjamin

[1] The men of Israel had sworn an oath at Mizpah: "None of us will give his daughter to a Benjaminite in marriage." [2] So the people went to Bethel and sat there before God until evening. They wept loudly and bitterly, [3] and cried out, "Why, LORD God of Israel, has it occurred that one tribe is missing in Israel today?" [4] The next day the people got up early, built an altar there, and offered burnt offerings and fellowship offerings. [5] The Israelites asked, "Who of all the tribes of Israel didn't come to the LORD with the assembly?" For a great oath had been taken that anyone who had not come to the LORD at Mizpah would certainly be put to death.

[6] But the Israelites had compassion on their brothers, the Benjaminites, and said, "Today a tribe has been cut off from Israel. [7] What should we do about wives for the survivors? We've sworn to the LORD not to give them any of our daughters as wives." [8] They asked, "Which city among the tribes of Israel didn't come to the LORD at Mizpah?" It turned out that no one from Jabesh-gilead had come to the camp and the assembly.

⁹ For when the roll was called, no men were there from the inhabitants of Jabesh-gilead.

¹⁰ The congregation sent twelve thousand brave warriors there and commanded them, "Go and kill the inhabitants of Jabesh-gilead with the sword, including women and dependents. ¹¹ This is what you should do: Completely destroy every male, as well as every woman who has gone to bed with a man." ¹² They found among the inhabitants of Jabesh-gilead four hundred young virgins, who had not been intimate with a man, and they brought them to the camp at Shiloh in the land of Canaan.

¹³ The whole congregation sent a message of peace to the Benjaminites who were at Rimmon Rock. ¹⁴ Benjamin returned at that time, and Israel gave them the women they had kept alive from Jabesh-gilead. But there were not enough for them.

¹⁵ The people had compassion on Benjamin, because the LORD had made this gap in the tribes of Israel. ¹⁶ The elders of the congregation said, "What should we do about wives for those who are left, since the women of Benjamin have been destroyed?" ¹⁷ They said, "There must be heirs for the survivors of Benjamin, so that a tribe of Israel will not be wiped out. ¹⁸ But we can't give them our daughters as wives." For the Israelites had sworn, "Anyone who gives a wife to a Benjaminite is cursed." ¹⁹ They also said, "Look, there's an annual festival to the LORD in Shiloh, which is north of Bethel, east of the highway that goes up from Bethel to Shechem, and south of Lebonah."

²⁰ Then they commanded the Benjaminites, "Go and hide in the vineyards. ²¹ Watch, and when you see the young women of Shiloh come out to perform the dances, each of you leave the vineyards and catch a wife for yourself from the young women of Shiloh, and go to the land of Benjamin. ²² When their fathers or brothers come to us and protest, we will tell them, 'Show favor to them, since we did not get enough wives for each of them in the battle. You didn't actually give the women to them, so you are not guilty of breaking your oath.'"

²³ The Benjaminites did this and took the number of women they needed from the dancers they caught. They went back to their own inheritance, rebuilt their cities, and lived in them. ²⁴ At that time, each of the Israelites returned from there to his own tribe and family. Each returned from there to his own inheritance.

²⁵ In those days there was no king in Israel; everyone did whatever seemed right to him.

DEUTERONOMY 12:8–12

[8] You are not to do as we are doing here today; everyone is doing whatever seems right in his own sight. [9] Indeed, you have not yet come into the resting place and the inheritance the LORD your God is giving you. [10] When you cross the Jordan and live in the land the LORD your God is giving you to inherit, and he gives you rest from all the enemies around you and you live in security, [11] then the LORD your God will choose the place to have his name dwell. Bring there everything I command you: your burnt offerings, sacrifices, offerings of the tenth, personal contributions, and all your choice offerings you vow to the LORD. [12] You will rejoice before the LORD your God—you, your sons and daughters, your male and female slaves, and the Levite who is within your city gates, since he has no portion or inheritance among you.

JAMES 3:13–18

The Wisdom from Above

[13] Who among you is wise and understanding? By his good conduct he should show that his works are done in the gentleness that comes from wisdom. [14] But if you have bitter envy and selfish ambition in your heart, don't boast and deny the truth. [15] Such wisdom does not come down from above but is earthly, unspiritual, demonic. [16] For where there is envy and selfish ambition, there is disorder and every evil practice.

[17] But the wisdom from above is first pure, then peace-loving, gentle, compliant, full of mercy and good fruits, unwavering, without pretense.

[18] And the fruit of righteousness is sown in peace by those who cultivate peace.

NOTES

27 / 28

GRACE DAY

Take this day to catch up on your reading, pray, and rest in the presence of the Lord.

Each Saturday we have turned from the tragedy of Judges to the hope of the gospel in Psalm 32, a psalm about joy and forgiveness.

PSALM 32:8–11

I will instruct you and show you
   the way to go;
with my eye on you, I will give counsel.
Do not be like a horse or mule,
without understanding,
that must be controlled with bit
   and bridle
or else it will not come near you.

Many pains come to the wicked,
but the one who trusts in the LORD
will have faithful love surrounding him.
Be glad in the LORD and rejoice,
you righteous ones;
shout for joy,
all you upright in heart.

Scripture is God-breathed and true. When we memorize it,
we carry His Word with us wherever we go.

For this study we have worked to memorize Judges 2:11–12a.
Spend some time reviewing the whole passage. As you do,
remember the weight of Israel's sin and rebellion, reflecting on
how our sin carries the same destructive power in our lives.

JUDGES 2:11–12a

[11] The Israelites did what was evil in the Lord's sight. They worshiped the Baals [12] and abandoned the Lord, the God of their ancestors, who had brought them out of Egypt.

See tips for memorizing Scripture on page 124.

BENEDICTION

MICAH 6:8

Mankind, he has told each of you what is good and what it is the LORD requires of you: to act justly, to love faithfulness, and to walk humbly with your God.

Tips for Memorizing Scripture

At She Reads Truth, we believe Scripture memorization is an important discipline in your walk with God. Committing God's Truth to memory means He can minister to us—and we can minister to others—through His Word no matter where we are. As you approach the Weekly Truth passage in this book, try these memorization tips to see which techniques work best for you!

STUDY IT

Study the passage in its biblical context and ask yourself a few questions before you begin to memorize it: What does this passage say? What does it mean? How would I say this in my own words? What does it teach me about God? Understanding what the passage means helps you know why it is important to carry it with you wherever you go.

Break the passage into smaller sections, memorizing a phrase at a time.

PRAY IT

Use the passage you are memorizing as a prompt for prayer.

WRITE IT

Dedicate a notebook to Scripture memorization and write the passage over and over again.

Diagram the passage after you write it out. Place a square around the verbs, underline the nouns, and circle any adjectives or adverbs. Say the passage aloud several times, emphasizing the verbs as you repeat it. Then do the same thing again with the nouns, then the adjectives and adverbs.

Write out the first letter of each word in the passage somewhere you can reference it throughout the week as you work on your memorization.

Use a whiteboard to write out the passage. Erase a few words at a time as you continue to repeat it aloud. Keep erasing parts of the passage until you have it all committed to memory.

CREATE

If you can, make up a tune for the passage to sing as you go about your day, or try singing it to the tune of a favorite song.

Sketch the passage, visualizing what each phrase would look like in the form of a picture. Or, try using calligraphy or altering the style of your handwriting as you write it out.

Use hand signals or signs to come up with associations for each word or phrase and repeat the movements as you practice.

SAY IT

Repeat the passage out loud to yourself as you are going through the rhythm of your day—getting ready, pouring your coffee, waiting in traffic, or making dinner.

Listen to the passage read aloud to you.

Record a voice memo on your phone and listen to it throughout the day or play it on an audio Bible.

SHARE IT

Memorize the passage with a friend, family member, or mentor. Spontaneously challenge each other to recite the passage, or pick a time to review your passage and practice saying it from memory together.

Send the passage as an encouraging text to a friend, testing yourself as you type to see how much you have memorized so far.

KEEP AT IT!

Set reminders on your phone to prompt you to practice your passage.

Purchase a She Reads Truth 12 Card Set or keep a stack of note cards with Scripture you are memorizing by your bed. Practice reciting what you've memorized previously before you go to sleep, ending with the passages you are currently learning. If you wake up in the middle of the night, review them again instead of grabbing your phone. Read them out loud before you get out of bed in the morning.

CSB BOOK ABBREVIATIONS

OLD TESTAMENT

GN Genesis	**JB** Job	**HAB** Habakkuk	**PHP** Philippians
EX Exodus	**PS** Psalms	**ZPH** Zephaniah	**COL** Colossians
LV Leviticus	**PR** Proverbs	**HG** Haggai	**1TH** 1 Thessalonians
NM Numbers	**EC** Ecclesiastes	**ZCH** Zechariah	**2TH** 2 Thessalonians
DT Deuteronomy	**SG** Song of Solomon	**MAL** Malachi	**1TM** 1 Timothy
JOS Joshua	**IS** Isaiah		**2TM** 2 Timothy
JDG Judges	**JR** Jeremiah	**NEW TESTAMENT**	**TI** Titus
RU Ruth	**LM** Lamentations	**MT** Matthew	**PHM** Philemon
1SM 1 Samuel	**EZK** Ezekiel	**MK** Mark	**HEB** Hebrews
2SM 2 Samuel	**DN** Daniel	**LK** Luke	**JMS** James
1KG 1 Kings	**HS** Hosea	**JN** John	**1PT** 1 Peter
2KG 2 Kings	**JL** Joel	**AC** Acts	**2PT** 2 Peter
1CH 1 Chronicles	**AM** Amos	**RM** Romans	**1JN** 1 John
2CH 2 Chronicles	**OB** Obadiah	**1CO** 1 Corinthians	**2JN** 2 John
EZR Ezra	**JNH** Jonah	**2CO** 2 Corinthians	**3JN** 3 John
NEH Nehemiah	**MC** Micah	**GL** Galatians	**JD** Jude
EST Esther	**NAH** Nahum	**EPH** Ephesians	**RV** Revelation

BIBLIOGRAPHY

Geoffrey W. Bromiley, ed., "Religions of the Biblical World: Canaanite (Syria and Palestine)." In *The International Standard Bible Encyclopedia, Revised*. Grand Rapids: Wm. B. Eerdmans, 1979–1988.

John D. Barry, ed., "Canaanite Religion." In *Lexham Bible Dictionary*, edited by John D. Barry et al. Bellingham: Lexham Press, 2016.

Get the Door
It's Truth

The **She Reads Truth Subscription Box** is an easy way to have a Bible reading plan delivered every month.

We'll send you a book filled with daily Scripture readings and all sorts of extra features to help you read and understand the Bible. All you have to do is open your book, read with us today, and read with us again tomorrow—it's that simple!

**beauty
goodness
truth**

You just spent 28 days in the Word of God!

THE DAY I THOUGHT
ABOUT THE MOST:

ONE THING I LEARNED
ABOUT GOD:

WHAT WAS GOD DOING IN
MY LIFE DURING THIS STUDY?

HOW DID I FIND DELIGHT IN GOD'S WORD?

WHAT DID I LEARN THAT I WANT TO SHARE
WITH SOMEONE ELSE?

A SPECIFIC PASSAGE OR VERSE
THAT ENCOURAGED ME:

A SPECIFIC PASSAGE OR VERSE THAT
CHALLENGED AND CONVICTED ME: